D0777361

Also by Anthony E. Wolf, Ph.D.

Mom, Jason's Breathing on Me!
THE SOLUTION TO SIBLING BICKERING

Get Out of My Life, but First Could You Drive Me and Cheryl to the Mall?
A PARENT'S GUIDE TO THE NEW TEENAGER

It's Not Fair, Jeremy Spencer's Parents Let Him Stay Up All Night!
A GUIDE TO THE TOUGHER PARTS OF PARENTING

Why Did You Have to Get a Divorce? And When Can I Have a Hamster?
A GUIDE TO PARENTING THROUGH DIVORCE

The Secret of Parenting: How to Be in Charge of Today's Kids— from Toddlers to Preteens—Without Threats or Punishment

I'll Be Home Before Midnight and I Won't Get Pregnant

Why Can't You Shut Up?

Why Can't You Shut Up?

*How We Ruin Relationships–
How Not To*

Anthony E. Wolf, Ph.D.

BALLANTINE BOOKS | NEW YORK

Published in the United States by Ballantine Books,
an imprint of The Random House Publishing Group,
a division of Random House, Inc., New York.

BALLANTINE and colophon are registered
trademarks of Random House, Inc.

Library of Congress Cataloging-in-Publication Data

Wolf, Anthony E.
    Why can't you shut up? : how we ruin relationships—how not to / Anthony E. Wolf.
        p. cm.
    ISBN 0-345-46093-6 (acid-free paper)
    1. Interpersonal relations. 2. Interpersonal communication. I. Title.

HM1106.W63 2006
158.2—dc22

                                                            2005057060

Printed in the United States of America on acid-free paper

www.ballantinebooks.com

9 8 7 6 5 4 3 2 1

First Edition

Book design by Mary A. Wirth

To Mary Alice

ACKNOWLEDGMENTS

I would like to thank Cynthia Merman and Elisabeth Kallick Dyssegaard for their help in editing drafts of this book. I want to thank Susanna Porter for her very thoughtful and rigorous editing of the final drafts that has made this a much better book than it would have been. I would like to thank Johanna Bowman for her ever-willing help in moving the book forward. As always, I want to thank my agent, Joe Spieler, without whom I would not have a career as a writer.

I also want to thank Sara Meiklejohn for her thoughtful advice with various stages of the book, and John Meiklejohn for his support and advice. I want to thank Diane Nadeau for helping to type many of the stages of this manuscript. I also want to thank Julie Vaillancourt for tolerating the gentleman with the stacks of papers at the Starbucks across the street from my office where most of this book was written.

I particularly want to thank my good friend Hugh Conlon for being a constantly willing and supportive listener in the writing of the book. Last, I want to thank my wife, Mary Alice, who has listened to or read—sometimes more than once—everything that has gone into this book, and for her continuing patience and support.

CONTENTS

FOREWORD

I am a practicing psychologist who throughout my professional life has worked with children, adolescents, and adults. I have been married to my wife, Mary Alice, for thirty-seven years. We have two grown children. As anybody who has been married or lives with a partner for an extended period of time knows, thirty-seven years is an incredibly long time for two people to stay together. Thirty-seven years is a lot of life. It is breathtaking to me, and I believe to Mary Alice as well, that we've been such a huge part of each other's lives for so long a time. I should add that we are both strong-willed people. Actually very strong willed. And on many issues we have disagreed. Many issues.

How, then, did we stay together?

There is a simple explanation. Though strong willed, I am also a wonderful, humble, and flexible person. I cannot tell you how many times in the course of our marriage it was I who gave in when I knew, and I mean *knew*, I was right and that Mary Alice was wrong. In fact, not only was I right, not only was Mary Alice wrong—I can show you videotapes and let you decide for yourself—but not once did Mary Alice recognize that I was right and she was wrong. Not one time. And not only did Mary Alice not concede I was right, she always said I was wrong. Often I would draw up extensive and clearly prepared legal briefs proving my case beyond any doubt. Mary Alice wouldn't even look at them.

"You should see yourself," was what she would usually say.

What did she mean by that? I didn't get it.

At parties, I would corner people. In supermarket lines—particularly where there were middle-aged lady cashiers—I would present my case, and invariably they would agree with me. In truth, the teenage cashiers and baggers weren't really so interested.

The point: Despite my having been right so many times, Mary Alice so wildly wrong, despite her so repeatedly maintaining just the opposite, we are still married. How could that be?

The answer is that somewhere in my brain—despite all that I have just said, despite all the obvious rightness of all the positions that I have taken and absolutely not convinced Mary Alice of—there has been another voice, a voice that spoke very differently. It spoke of a very important fact: I actually like this relationship. I love my wife. I think I am unbelievably lucky. I don't want the relationship to end. Not only that, I want the time that Mary Alice and I are together to be as nice as possible. I'm lucky that Mary Alice puts up with me—has put up with me for all these years.

Somehow, enough of the time, that saner voice came through.

Another point: Thinking back about all those times that I was right, I don't actually remember exactly what it was that I was so right about.

But it is also true that there were times when the saner voice did not come through. There were many times when my less mature side *did* win out. And those times were not so good.

This book is about the constant battle between the part of us that is reasonable and actually has as its top priority what is genuinely best for us and for our relationships, and on the other side, a very primitive part in all of us, a part that has a great power, a part whose only interest is getting its way *now*. And in that pursuit, it never backs down, never lets go, and with complete disregard for its own best interests will wreck relationships to achieve its own primitive goal.

I call it the baby self.

Why Can't You Shut Up?

Presenting the Baby Self

At work, a box of doughnuts was passed around, but Kathleen, who was watching her weight, didn't have any. *I really shouldn't,* she thought.

However, that evening Kathleen didn't think anything as she polished off the six doughnuts she had picked up on the way home from work for the family's breakfast the next morning.

Robert had a reputation for always being courteous with clients and co-workers.

However, at home with his family he was often rude, short-tempered, and impatient, an entirely less mature, far less pleasant person.

———

Arnold spent Saturday afternoon at his friend Hugh's house helping him put up shelving in his basement.

However, it was now four months since Arnold had promised his wife that he would fix the cabinet in the downstairs bathroom. "I will. If you just don't keep bugging me about it. I said I would do it."

Claire, at thirty-eight, had reached a level of hard-won maturity; she could deal with even the most difficult interpersonal situations with real poise.

But her mother had only to open her mouth and Claire found herself feeling and acting like a six-year-old.

We all have two distinct modes of operating, really two separate selves. Both are us. Both are necessary. One—what I call the baby self—is the mode of basic nurturing. The baby self likes to be home, relax, and unwind. It wants to be fed now, and it tolerates absolutely no stress. It has no patience, no self-control. It just wants what it wants. It is the side of us that likes to sit on the couch, watch TV, eat Doritos, and be bothered by nothing and nobody.

"Honey, could you hand me the remote?"

"It's right next to you."

"But I'll have to stretch a little to reach it, and you know about my back."

"No, I don't know about your back. This is the first I've heard of it."

"Well, now you do. Could you hand me the remote? Please."

But there is another side to us—what I call the mature self—that operates at a completely different, much higher level. This part of us is willing to go out into the world, work, postpone gratification, and deal with stress to accomplish goals. It has patience, and it has self-control. These two modes exist side by side. Over the course of a day, they operate very much like a shifting of gears. Sometimes one is in control, sometimes the other.

Our baby selves tend to come out at home and especially in the presence of those in our lives to whom we are closest and with whom we feel the most comfortable. Immediate family members bring out our baby self—our partners, our children, our siblings, often our parents. But so do close friends. And, of course, roommates, regardless of whether they are friends or not. Last and most inconvenient—our baby self can surface with bosses and co-workers. Bosses have real power over us, so work can mimic the family—boss as the parent, co-workers as siblings.

All baby selves are the same. They do not vary from person to person, and they do not change over time. Adult baby selves remain just as babyish as they always were. They remain a part of us throughout our lives. But the mature self does change. It grows, and gradually it takes over our day-to-day behavior until it controls—at least some of the time—the urgings of our baby self.

However, babyish as it is, the baby self has a major positive role in our lives. It is only in the baby self mode that we can get the deep nurturing we need for our sense of well-being and happiness. I picture it like a boxer between rounds. He's been out in the ring, done what he must, but then he returns to his corner to collapse and get some rest. Once replenished, he heads out again. Without some place in our lives for baby self nurturing, life would be all work and no fun. Our stress levels would be intolerably high.

Baby self nurturing comes from the basic pleasures in life: eating, sex, sleeping, and watching *I Love Lucy* reruns. But also, and perhaps most important, it comes from interacting with those we love—close friends, family, partners. Starting in childhood, we learn that to get along in the world, we need to present a more polite, controlled, better-behaved version of ourselves. It is the public version of us. But our other side—our baby self, both the good and the bad—is reserved for those with whom we can most fully "be ourselves." It is with them that we form our most meaningful attachments. Those deeper bonds grow only when our baby self can be part of the relationship as well.

But what that means is that once we are truly engaged in a strong, potentially long-term relationship, the less than wonderful side of our baby self makes itself known (if it has not already). Baby selves are warm, affectionate, funny, spontaneous—all the characteristics that make for strong, enjoyable, close relationships. But so too because they are *baby* selves, when not getting their way they can be quite unpleasant—demanding, bossy, selfish, lazy in the extreme. For that relationship to give us the deepest long-term pleasure, our baby self side must have a place within that relationship. But this means that once a close relationship is allowed to fully develop, the not-so-nice parts of the baby self will make their appearance. There can be surprises.

"I don't understand. Before we started living together, George was always ready to help me if I needed anything done. But since we've been living together, I can't get him to do anything. It's like he's a different person."

"I don't understand. Before we got engaged, Melissa was so easy to please. Whatever I wanted to do seemed to be okay with her. But since we've gotten engaged, everything has to be exactly her way. She's a different person."

It is the paradox of baby selves and intimate relationships. We care about our loved ones the most, but precisely *because* of the closeness, they get our baby self much more than others in our lives. It is the main challenge for any close relationship: including your baby self without having it ruin the relationship.

The Biggest Problem About Baby Selves

Because it is a *baby* self, some of what it wants doesn't work well in adult life. It is infinitely lazy, extremely bossy, mindlessly piggy, and heedless of others. It cannot be satisfied with some; it wants everything. It wants total control. But the biggest problem in adult life, especially in relationships, is that the baby self, when not getting its way, doesn't know how to let go. It does not know when to back off.

"Do you have any idea where I put my little scissors?"

"How am I supposed to know?"

"I was just asking."

"Well, it's not my job to keep track of all your stuff."

"I'm sorry, I was just wondering if you had seen the little scissors."

"I would have told you if I'd seen them, wouldn't I?"

"You don't have to get nasty."

"I'm not getting nasty."

"You are getting nasty."

"You're crazy. I just said I didn't know where your scissors were."

"You should hear your tone of voice."

"You should hear *your* tone of voice. I can't even talk to you without you always getting offended."

"You don't understand how you come across."

"What? It's bitch at Larry time again?"

How did I get into this? I was just wondering if he'd seen my little scissors.

There is nothing that damages relationships so regularly as that one part in all of us that cannot move on. Nothing else comes close. So often in our lives—contrary to what we want—we damage and even cause the end of relationships with partners, friends, relatives, and co-workers. When anything negative enters the relationship—a disagreement, an unkind word, a perceived slight—there is a part in all of us that cannot move forward, unless that bad feeling is completely removed, unless whatever was negative gets completely resolved.

Inside us, the voice of our baby self never backs off:

I have to get her to see my way.

I have to get her to understand.

We have to get some kind of resolution to this.

We can't just leave it hanging like this.

So rather than disengage, we get in deeper and deeper.

"But you don't understand."

"*I'm* the one who doesn't understand? *I'm* the one? What about the time at Madeline and Phil's? What about that?"

"What about that? What about last summer at your father's?"

"Don't you dare get into that!"

"Why not? It's okay for you to talk about the time with me and Lucille."

"You just better watch it."

"*You* better watch it."

As a result, instead of moving on and allowing time and distance to lay the hurt to rest, we persist and make it worse.

This need not to let go is so much a part of us, so deep and so powerful, that despite the way it often hurts us, it controls much of how we choose to act. It develops its own voice. It is a voice that learns to fool the more logical part of us—our mature self—with excuses why we cannot, should not, let go of an argument. We believe these false reasons are good, right, correct, what we must do. But they are not correct at all. They are the primitive urgings of that part of us whose only want, whose unvarying demand, is to get its way; unless it does, it will never move on. So for what we invariably think are valid reasons, we create unnecessary problems.

This book is about how not to have your baby self run your life and wreck your relationships. It is a guide to the baby self: what it is, how it thinks and acts, and how it influences your life, good and bad. I will teach you to recognize the baby self's voice inside you and to distinguish what is truly mature and reasonable from what only seems to be. As a result, you will learn to act in ways that will make your life and relationships better.

In what follows, I will teach you how to avoid being pulled into those arguments that you do not seek in the first place, normal conversations that inexplicably go awry. I will give you rules for conducting good arguments and avoiding bad ones. And I will present the many false reasons we give ourselves as to why we should hold on when we should not. This book will let you train yourself to resist the unhelpful urgings of your baby self and so avoid many of the pitfalls that sabotage relationships.

And I will present a very useful phenomenon: Only when you accept that having a baby self is part of being a human, only then can you see its hand, its influence behind so much of how you think. You don't have to hate your baby self. But you don't always have to give in to its demands, either.

More About Your Baby Self

If you are going to recognize the influence of your baby self, it is obviously useful to know it. So before I describe how to deal with it so that it doesn't create too much havoc in your life, let me briefly describe the basic characteristics of all baby selves.

The Baby Self Is Self-Centered, Piggy, and Clueless

The baby self sits at the core of a universe that exists only to fulfill its needs. It genuinely does not understand that others could exist in their own right and have legitimate wants as well.

"You took all the chocolate cupcakes. You know I like the chocolate ones, too. What about me?"

"What about you?"

The baby self doesn't get it. The baby self in us genuinely does not understand that others' needs have any validity or relevance.

It was Clarissa's thirtieth birthday party. Janelle was not having fun. Everybody was paying attention to Clarissa, and Clarissa was loving it, soaking up the attention.

What about me? screamed Janelle's baby self. *I'm cool. I have lots of interesting things to say. Clarissa's all surface and boring compared to me. Hello! Everybody! Hello! Over here!*

Oh, just shut up, intruded Janelle's mature self. *Clarissa's getting the attention because it's her birthday. The party is about her. That's what happens at birthday parties. They are about the person who's having the birthday. There are 364 other days when you can outcharm her. It is her birthday party. Just shut up and have more cake.*

But I want people to pay attention to me. It's not fair.

Just shut up.

And in this instance, Janelle's mature self ruled. She did shut up. And she did not accidentally spill hot coffee on her arm so that the attention would be drawn to her, although the thought occurred to her. But she didn't have a good time.

You did good, said Janelle's mature self to her baby self. *I hate you,* said Janelle's baby self to her mature self.

The baby self wants everything. It craves not just what it needs, but all it can get. The baby self does not know the meaning of "some" or "enough."

How much money does one need to spend on a mountain bike?

How elaborate a birthday party does one need to have for a two-year-old?

How many crystal paper weights are enough?

The baby self has no capacity to look at itself, no self-awareness, no conscience. It just feels, sees, and wants.

I'm not pretty, I'm not ugly. I'm not smart, I'm not stupid. I'm not good, I'm not bad. I just am.

Obviously this is a nice way to be because it allows us to relax. But it is also why, when in our baby self mode, we can at times act like such jerks. This is also why we can act and feel so differently depending on our surroundings.

I'm really getting fat. Whenever I go to the mall, I feel so self-conscious. But at home, when it is just family, I don't worry about how I look at all. I'm home.

I can't possibly go to that party with those doctors Karen knows from work. I won't have anything to say. Everybody will think I'm stupid.

But at home, he is Mr. Know-It-All, not caring in the least that everybody there always calls him an idiot, their put-downs not slowing him down one bit. *"You're* all idiots, you just don't know it."

———

In surroundings that bring out our baby self, we are just us.

Because the baby self lacks self-awareness, many common human emotions are simply not part of its repertoire: shame, guilt, embarrassment—and pride.

"Richard, aren't you embarrassed walking around the house looking like such a slob?"

"Huh?"

Not the baby self.

The Baby Self Lives for the Present

The baby self exists only in the now. This is why arguing with one can be so frustrating. It can recall its past, but it owns none of it. It's like watching a movie. *Yes, I can see that was me in the picture. But that was then.* The baby self feels no responsibility for its actions.

"Don't you remember throwing all my opera CDs in the driveway and then driving over them?"

"Well, yes, I can picture in my head the event happening, and I can hear the CDs crunching under the tires. But that was then. I am truly sorry about your CDs, but if you have a problem with the person who ruined them, you'll have to take it up with him."

"But that was you, asshole."

"Yes, it *was* me. But it's not me now."

This *is* how the baby self thinks.

"You really are an asshole."

"I wish you wouldn't swear so much."

The baby self feels no responsibility for its past—or for its future.

"So, Louie, when are you going to fix the garage door?"

"Tonight. I'll fix it tonight. I swear to God."

"Louie, you always say that."

"Yeah, but this time I mean it."

And Louie *does* mean it. In his heart he means it. But at that moment, he doesn't have to do it. Later, that other guy will fix the garage door. The other guy who later, of course, doesn't.

"But you said you would do it."

"Yeah, I didn't understand how I would feel now. Really, I'm so tired and my back's acting up again."

The Baby Self's One Big Worry

This book will pay particular attention to one great worry that plagues all baby selves. It is this worry, beyond all else, that is at the heart of why we so often get enmeshed in arguments and cannot move on.

Early in a child's life, its basic source of nurturing and security is Mommy or Daddy. The baby self is engulfed within their protecting arms.

As long as I am connected to Mommy or Daddy, there are no worries. They will take care of me.

The baby self's sole concern—in childhood, but in adult life, too—is that it must feel at all times connected to its main source of love and security. The baby self hates being alone more than anything else.

If I am alone, if I am truly on my own, then it becomes tiny little me out there at the mercy of a giant random universe over which I have no control and which does not care about me in the least.

In Greek mythology, there was a man named Antaeus. Because he was the son of the goddess of the earth, as long as Antaeus's feet were on the ground, connected to Mother Earth, he was infinitely strong and invincible. He could not be defeated. Hercules, the Greek superman, had to fight him. And, strong as Hercules was, he could not beat Antaeus until he lifted him off the ground, separating him from the source of his strength and invincibility.

The baby self must always feel connected to its basic source of safety and nurturing. Aloneness, vulnerability, is exclusively the domain of the mature self. Aloneness, above all else, is the enemy of the baby self. More intolerable to a baby self than anything is feeling a loss of connection to that ultimate source of love and security. Particularly the case with our strongest love connections, this also applies in any and all human interactions.

I cannot overemphasize the power of this aspect of the baby self in our adult lives. With any interaction with another fellow human where there is even the slightest discord, the baby self in us will not tolerate letting go unless there is total agreement. So it is that even with the simplest, most straightforward interactions, we so often inexplicably find ourselves drawn into these escalating battles that we never sought to begin with but somehow cannot seem to leave alone until perfect harmony is once again restored. Unfortunately, in many real-life situations this plan does not work so well.

Why can't we shut up? Stupidly, self-defeatingly, why do we have to pick up on *everything*? Why can't we let even the slightest unpleasant comment pass? Why must we work everything through to death, where all that ever does is make things worse? What is wrong with us? It is the hardest thing about being an adult. There are times where we truly must be on our own.

Part I

What to Do

Chapter 1

The Rules for
Better Communication

The baby self plays havoc with day-to-day conversations. In what follows, I will describe the basic rules for better communication. Let me start with simple exchanges in which someone wants to convey a specific piece of information:

> "Please pass the salt."
> "I'm sorry I'm late."
> "I think it's going to rain."

The problem is that you offer a simple statement, but the person to whom you are speaking has something more to say:

> "Please pass the salt."
> "Why can't you reach it yourself?"

———— ⸳

"I'm sorry I'm late."
"You're always late."

"I think it's going to rain."
"Like I care."

And in response to what this other person says, you feel the need to answer back:

"Please pass the salt."
"Why can't you reach it yourself?"
"Why can't I reach it myself?" (on an angry, incredulous note)

"I'm sorry I'm late."
"You're always late."
"I'm not always late."

"I think it's going to rain."
"Like I care."
"I was just trying to make conversation."

And then, of course, they respond to your response. And somehow you find yourself in a hole, the dialogue rapidly deteriorating back and forth:

"Please pass the salt."
"Why can't you reach it yourself?"
"Why can't I reach it myself?"
"Yeah, you're the one who wants the salt."
"What is your problem? Why do you have to be difficult on purpose?"
"What is *your* problem?"

————

"I'm sorry I'm late."

"You're always late."

"I'm not always late."

"You *are* always late."

"You're exaggerating."

"No. What about last Thursday? What about when I was supposed to meet you at the Cloningers'?"

"I think it's going to rain."

"Like I care."

"I was just trying to make conversation."

"Like I care."

"I was just trying to make conversation. That's all I was doing."

"Why do you always feel you have to make conversation?"

The problem here is that their response to what you say makes you feel that you *have to* respond to what they have just said. You *cannot* just let it pass. But that is exactly what you need to do. The rules are simple: *Stay on the subject—your subject. Do not be led astray by what you may feel are provocative responses. Then disengage.*

"Please pass the salt."

"Why can't you reach it yourself?"

But then, not picking up on the rude response, either reach for the salt yourself or repeat the request.

"Would you please pass the salt?"

Most of the time, unless they are choosing to be *very* difficult, they usually—ungraciously—will pass the salt.

"Thank you."

"I'm sorry I'm late."

"You're always late."

And not defending yourself:

"I'm sorry."
Then say no more.

"I think it's going to rain."
"Like I care."
Here it is best to say nothing. You've attempted to make conversation, and they obviously aren't interested. Why would you possibly want to continue?

Of course, in reading what I just recommended, part of you probably agrees, but part of you is saying: *But I can't. I can't just not respond to what they said. I can't simply let them say what they said and say nothing.*

But again, that is exactly what I am recommending, if your aim is to have conversations that ultimately go forward in more positive directions.

Useful and Not Useful Ways of Communicating

The rules for more positive outcomes in basic communication are simple. In a discussion, as soon as you start to feel yourself getting irritated—which is a signal that your baby self is getting caught up with the other person's baby self—you need to disengage. Say what you have to say and end the conversation. Stay on track; do not respond to side issues. If you feel that what they bring up cries for a response, don't do it then. Wait until later, at an emotionally neutral time and—if you still care enough to get back to it—bring it up then.

This is easy to understand but not so easy to do, because there is so much inside of you that screams, *You have to answer them!* But all that ever does is drag you in deeper. Once baby selves lock horns, fast disengagement is always best. Once baby selves engage, *anything* further that you might say only pours fuel on the fire. You may *feel* strongly that you cannot let it go, but remember that your baby self literally fears, cannot tolerate, disengagement. It will never let you move on. But you must.

The following dialogues have two versions. In the first, the baby self dominates and the discussion goes progressively downhill. In the second, early on one of the protagonists disengages, with far better results.

Not so good:

"Valerie, I don't see why you can't go to Sally's baby shower."

"Mother, I already told you. My boss asked me to work that weekend, and at this point at work, I'm not comfortable saying no."

"But she's your sister."

"I know that, Mother. I already apologized to her, and she understood."

"But she feels hurt."

"She doesn't feel hurt. She said she understood."

"That's what she said to you. But I know how she feels. She always felt that you didn't really care about her."

"I do care about Sally. I just can't go to her shower."

"No, you think you do, but you've always ignored her. I don't know why."

"I don't ignore Sally. Don't you remember how I took time off from work when she had her operation?"

"She feels that you look down on her because she didn't finish college."

"I don't look down on her."

"If you miss her baby shower, it will just be further proof to her that you don't care."

"Mother! I do care about Sally."

"Well, you certainly have a funny way of showing it."

Better:

"Valerie, I don't see why you can't go to Sally's baby shower."

"Mother, I already told you. My boss asked me to work that weekend, and at this point at work, I'm not comfortable saying no."

"But she's your sister."

"I'm sorry, but I can't go."

"But she feels hurt that you always ignore her."

Here Valerie must disengage.

"Mother, I'm sorry, but I am not going."

"You just don't see how you have always hurt Sally."

"Gosh, Mother. I don't know what to say."

"You don't even realize it."

"I'll talk to you later."

"You really should reconsider. She is your sister."

"Good-bye, Mother. I love you a lot."

Valerie does not want to get into an emotionally loaded discussion with her mother about whether she has always ignored her sister. Valerie has let her mother know that she won't be going to the baby shower, and there is nothing more that she needs to say. Valerie may feel that she needs to convince her mother that she does care about her sister, but this is not the time. If she keeps talking, she'll just become increasingly frustrated.

Wouldn't it be nice if:

"Gosh, Valerie, now that you've explained it to me, I can see how I was wrong. You do care about Sally. And of course I understand about your missing the shower because of pressure from work. It's just your silly old mom, fussing again."

But of course that kind of mature reconciliation tends to happen only in our dreams.

Similar rules apply with unpleasant teasing. Consider the following two exchanges.

Not so good:

"Hey, funny ears."

"Marco, you know I hate it when you call me that."

"But, Tina, you do have funny ears."

"I know it's silly, but I'm sensitive about my ears. I don't like you calling me that."

"But I'm only kidding. Besides, your funny ears are kind of cute—for funny ears."

"Marco, I asked you to stop."

"I'm only kidding. You're too sensitive."

"I can't help it. I hate it when you call me that."

"When I call you what? Say it."

"Marco. Stop it!"

"Stop what?"

Better:

"Hey, funny ears."

"Marco, please don't call me that. You know I don't like it."

"But, Tina, you do have funny ears."

At this point, or even when Marco first calls her "funny ears"—because he already knows that Tina doesn't like it—Tina should say no more. If he continues, she should leave. Teasing, like obscene phone calls, feeds off a response. The more Tina fusses at Marco about the teasing, the more he will continue to tease. It is nonresponse—and only nonresponse—that ultimately ends the unwanted behavior.

Later, but only later—and only if Tina is still irritated enough about the teasing to bring it up again:

"I don't like it when you call me 'funny ears.' I don't think it's funny. I don't want you to call me that ever again."

Note that this is not a discussion; it's a statement. Tina wants Marco to know that she does not like the teasing. She is not inviting a response from Marco. To the extent that she tries to make sure he understands, Tina only sets herself up for more negative back-and-forth with Marco.

It is not just words that pull us into an argument. Sometimes the speaker's attitude seems to demand immediate straightening out.

———

Not so good:

    Mother to her teenage daughter: "Marcia, please get in here."

    "What?" (Spoken in a very surly tone.)

    "Don't talk to me in that tone of voice."

    "What?"

    "I said I don't like that tone of voice."

    "What do you want?"

    "Marcia, do not be rude to me."

    "You're rude."

    "You're grounded."

    "Well, fuck you. I hate this house."

Marcia's mother never even got a chance to ask Marcia if she had remembered to clean the litter box.

Better:

    "Marcia, please get in here."

    "What?" (Spoken in a very surly tone.)

    "Marcia, did you remember to clean the litter box?" (Not picking up on Marcia's tone of voice)

    "I don't know."

    "Please check it, and if it needs changing, please change it." (Not "What do you mean, you don't know?")

    "Why do you always ask me to do stuff?"

    "Thank you, Marcia." (Not "I don't always ask you to do stuff. In fact, I ask you to do very little.")

    Again, if Marcia's mother wishes to speak to Marcia about her surly attitude, she can do so—later.

    "Marcia, when I ask you to do something, I don't want you always giving me a hard time about it."

    "I don't give you a hard time about it. You give me a hard time about it."

If at that point Marcia's mother says no more, Marcia has heard, and her mother's words will have an effect. It may not always look like it, but Marcia hears. She does care, even though she may wish she didn't. At that point, bringing up her daughter's surly attitude only invites counterattacks and definitely gets off the subject of litter boxes, thereby weakening her basic point.

Remember, the baby self is lazy. It would much rather create endless diversions than actually have to *do* anything.

Not so good:
    "Russell."
    "What?"
    "Did you remember to empty the litter box?"
    "Marlena, we should drown that stupid cat."
    "You said you would help me with it when we got Mr. Whiskers."
    "I don't like him. We should drown him."
    "We're not going to drown him. I'm sorry you don't like the cat."
    "Well, I don't. He smells."
    "He doesn't smell. We had him neutered."
    "I think we should get rid of him."
    Russell will go on forever because he would much rather argue than check the litter box, which would require effort.

Better:
    "Russell."
    "What?"
    "Did you remember to check the litter box?"
    "Marlena, we should drown that stupid cat."
    "Please check the litter box and see if it needs changing."
    "I hate that cat. I really do. It was a mistake getting it."
    "Thank you, Russell."
    Either Russell will or won't empty the litter box, but no way does Marlena want to get into a should-we-drown-the-cat discussion. She just wants Russell to check the litter box.

The same rule applies when giving advice as well. The most you can ever do with advice is give it. No matter how good the advice, no matter how right you are, the most you can ever do is say what you have to say as clearly and concisely as possible, and in the end the recipient of your excellent advice will take it or not. But the baby self is never satisfied with just *giving* advice, it wants to make sure that it's taken.

Not so good:

"Rick, I feel awful. I think I'm going to call in sick to work tomorrow."

"Sandi, I think you have to go. You've called in sick a lot lately."

"But I am sick."

"They don't care. They just want people they can rely on. I think you're risking getting fired."

"Listen, don't tell me what to do. I don't tell you what to do."

"Yes, you do. You tell me what to do all the time. Besides, I'm just saying this for your own good."

"Well, you know what? I'm an adult. I'm going to do what I'm going to do. Don't go bossing me around."

"I'm not bossing you around. I'm just stating a fact."

"A fact according to you. You think you know everything. You don't know shit."

"You're impossible. You're just a big baby."

"You can't stand it that I want to run my own life."

Better:

"Rick, I feel awful. I'm going to call in sick to work tomorrow."

"I think you have to go. You've called in sick a lot lately."

"But I am sick."

"They don't care. They just want people they can rely on. I think you're risking getting fired."

"Listen, don't tell me what to do. I don't tell you what to do."

At this point, Rick needs to end the conversation. He's made his statement, which has been met with resistance. Anything more he might say just takes away from the impact of his message.

"You just want to run my life. Well, I'm sorry, I'm not a kid. I'm going to do what I want to do."

Maybe Sandi will call in sick tomorrow and maybe she won't. But Rick has said all that he needs to.

Last, others who know us well can be quite skilled at bringing out our baby self. They bring up issues that resonate and might require scrutiny at another time and place. That is, they know how to use real issues to push our buttons. But the rule remains the same. Stay on the subject. Say what you have to say. Then disengage.

Not so good:

"Sam, I want to talk to you."

"What?"

"I think you need to be doing more for little Bobby."

"Oh, for chrissake, Mary Beth. Not this shit again. We've been over this a million times."

"I think you should give him supper on Tuesdays and Thursdays. It will be a break for me, and you'll be spending time doing stuff with him."

"I do plenty with him."

"No, you don't. You're home a lot, but all you do is watch TV. He's your kid, too."

At this point, Sam, not wanting to feed their two-year-old son on Tuesdays, Thursdays, or any day because it interferes with his TV watching, is searching desperately for something to keep the argument going. Finally he lights upon what he hopes will be a winner.

"You're just saying this because you have it in your head that Kenny [Mary Beth's brother] does more with Kenny Jr. than I do with Bobby. This always happens after we spend time with Kenny and Danielle." (This is partially true, because seeing her brother and Kenny Jr. does bring up the issue for Mary Beth.)

"This has nothing to do with Kenny and Kenny Jr."

"You know it does. Every time we go over there, it's the same thing."

"This has nothing to do with Kenny and Kenny Jr."

"The hell it doesn't. You know what? Kenny doesn't do any more with Kenny Jr. than I do with Bobby. You just got that in your head from one time when we were with them, and now it just comes into your head every time we see them."

"Well, actually Kenny does do more with Kenny Jr."

"I knew it was that. And no, he doesn't. You don't know what goes on most of the time. Kenny just likes to show off, do his look-what-a-good-dad-I-am bullshit whenever anybody's around."

"No, Danielle tells me he helps."

"Kenny has Danielle totally wrapped around his finger. She believes anything Kenny says."

"She's not like that."

"She is too."

Better:

"Sam, I want to talk to you."

"What?"

"I think you need to be doing more for little Bobby."

"Oh, for chrissake, Mary Beth, not this shit again."

"I want you to give him supper Tuesdays and Thursdays. It will be a break for me, and you'll be doing stuff with him."

"I do plenty with him."

Here, Mary Beth should not add fuel to the argument. She should repeat her statement, and that's it.

"I would like you to give Bobby supper on Tuesdays and Thursdays."

"This is bullshit. You just say this every time after we visit Danielle and Kenny."

To the extent that Mary Beth responds to Sam's counterarguments, she blunts the strength and focus of her request.

Sam probably knows that Mary Beth is right. He should do more with Bobby. He is reluctant to simply refuse, which might risk unknown countermeasures from Mary Beth. From Sam's standpoint, it is a far better strategy to argue than to say no.

From Mary Beth's standpoint, it is like a path that goes straight ahead but with many side branches; to the extent that she gets pulled off the main route, she loses. Though there is some truth in Sam's statement, the bottom line, which Mary Beth must stay with, is that she wants Sam to spend more time with their son, and she is making a proposal about Tuesday and Thursday suppers. Maybe Sam will go along with the request, maybe he won't. But the best thing to do, as always, is to say what you have to say and then end the discussion.

Chapter 2

Arguments—
Good Ones and Bad Ones

One summer early in our marriage, when Mary Alice was pregnant with Nick, our first child, we went on a vacation that involved a lot of driving. To this day, I can look at a map of the areas that we drove through and pick out the different towns where we had *really* big arguments (that is, *really* big, as opposed to the many more arguments we had that were not quite so big). We had been married for almost three years. But both of us felt that with a child coming, the added tie and commitment of being parents meant we were probably going to be together for many years.

What were the arguments about? I didn't mind driving with the windows up if that was what Mary Alice preferred. But was I willing to drive with the windows up *for the rest of my life?* I would rather drive an extra hour and wait until one o'clock to stop for lunch, but I was willing to stop at noon if that was what Mary Alice wanted. *But not for the next forty years.* Mary Alice could tolerate that I always walked at a pace that left her lagging behind. But she had no intention of tolerating it *for the next forty years.* Our baby selves had so far participated in the relationship, which was what had allowed it to be intimate and comfortable. But up until now, our baby selves had been willing to suppress many of their nonessential needs for the sake of furthering the relationship. Once they were faced with what might be a very long time, our baby selves made it very clear. *I don't think so. Not forever.*

Two people who are going to be together, spend a significant part of their lives in close contact with each other, share much of the same life space, are not always going to want the same thing. They will disagree. They will argue. Arguments are not bad; without conflict in a relationship, there is the risk that one or both partners sacrifice too much of how they truly feel or think. Without conflict, one person is either dominating the other, or both people are merely moving parallel through the same space, with no true connection.

But there are good arguments and there are bad arguments.

Zack and Rita have been living together for two years. One Saturday, a package arrived for Zack from Fast Water Inc.

"What's in the package?" asked Rita.

"Just something I ordered from a catalog months ago."

"What is it? Open it up. Is it a secret?" (Actually, it was a secret.)

"Of course not."

Zack opened the package. Inside was a new flyfishing rod.

"You already have two fly rods."

"I knew you were going to say that."

"How much did it cost?"

"Not much."

"How much is not much?"

Zack told her. It was more than not much.

"I can't believe you! You can spend money on a fishing rod that you don't need, and we still have our piece-of-shit couch."

"I knew this was going to happen."

"If you knew this was going to happen, why did you buy the fishing rod?"

"It's not the same thing as the couch. A couch costs ten times what I paid for the fishing rod."

"You don't understand. It's okay if it's something you want, but it's not okay if it's something I want. I just don't see why we can't afford to get a new couch."

"We've been through this before. Once we have the money for a place of our own, then we can start buying luxury items."

"Luxury items? Replacing a couch that belonged in the junkyard five years ago is not a luxury item. A third expensive fly rod is a luxury item."

"It's not the same thing."

"I hate our couch. You have this one-track mind; everything is about saving money so we can buy a house. I want to have a nice life now. I'm not going to have my life run by your obsession. And then you buy yourself another expensive fishing rod."

"I told you, it's not the same thing as a couch, and it's not an obsession. I don't want to spend a lot of money now. I work hard, and it really depresses me that time goes by and we're not getting ahead, we're not putting away any money. Buying a new couch would just push us backward."

"And spending money on a fly rod won't? I want to have a life."

"Did we need the whole new set of place mats you bought last week?"

"Don't you dare compare the two. The place mats hardly cost anything. And at least I can look at them instead of the ugly couch. Your fishing rod was expensive and you know it."

"I'll break the fishing rod, okay? I'm gonna fucking break it. I don't care about it now. I like something, and you have to spoil it."

"Great. Now I've ruined your one happy time, the one thing you love. You are such a baby."

"Well, fuck you!"

Zack turned and stormed out. Rita could hear his car start up, tires screeching as he drove away.

This was a good argument. In reality, it would have lasted a lot longer—half an hour, an hour, maybe more. But the content would have been similar, just more repetitious.

It was a good argument because it had the three basic "good argument" elements:

1. Each person got to say his or her piece.

    Rita got to state her main points: She thinks Zack has a one-sided policy about spending money—he can buy a fishing rod, she can't buy a couch. She very much wants a new couch, and she feels trapped by Zack's narrow-minded focus on saving money for a who-knows-when future.

    Zack got his say: He doesn't think that his getting a new fishing rod is such a big deal. He does not want to get a new couch, and it makes him depressed that he and Rita are not able to save money as fast as he would like.

2. Each person was heard.

    Both Zack and Rita were heard. Zack heard. Rita heard. Of course, the argument did not take the form of a calm, respectful give-and-take.

    "Gee, I don't like what you're saying, but I can see your point. Can you think of anything else that could help me to better see it from your perspective? Take your time."

    Not quite. When we are deep in an argument with someone to whom we are close, feelings are much more on the surface. Because of this, the other person's listening often sounds more like "No. No way. You don't understand." That is, they don't always shut up when we are talking, nor do we when they talk.

    But they do hear, they do listen. They may be yelling at you all the while, but they hear.

3. The argument ended.

    The discussion was ultimately closed.

That's it. In a good argument, both participants get to express clearly, fully, and strongly their side of the story—all of it. They are heard, and then the argument ends.

A good argument does not have to end in resolution. If that happens, great. But it's not a requirement. The vast majority of adult arguments between close friends or couples do not end with an instant solution.

Zack and Rita's was not a bad argument; it did not include the following:

1. The argument did not become violent—no hitting, no threats of physical violence (which for a man can happen simply if he stands too close to the person he is mad at).

2. Neither Zack nor Rita used cruel, demeaning language. There is a big difference between angry words that basically say, "I am very mad at you" (for example, "Jerk"; "I can't believe you're talking to me this way"; or "I hate you"), and cruel words that attack the character of the other person ("You're such a loser"; "You're pathetic"; "How many jobs have you been fired from?"; "You're disgusting, fat, and ugly"; "No wonder you have no friends"). To the recipient, they *feel* very different. Angry words make you feel angry. Demeaning words hit at your sense of self; they stay with you, sink in, and make you feel vulnerable and hurt.

3. Neither Zack nor Rita got overly sidetracked from the issue at hand: *who has a right to spend money on what, and when.* Neither brought up every grievance since the beginning of time:

   "What about when you ordered lobster at the Hanging Garden but made a big fuss when I ordered dessert?"

   "I'll tell you what's inconsiderate. Why does your mother have to come over every other Thursday regardless of whether it's convenient for me or not?"

   Nor did they—as so often happens in arguments—generalize from the specific to overall serious flaws in the relationship:

   "You're such a selfish person. Everything is about you. I think maybe the main reason I get depressed is that I'm giving up too much to keep our relationship going."

   Some of this is inevitable in a long emotional argument. But getting completely sidetracked changes the whole tenor of the discussion.

4. Neither of the participants was so stuck that they could not allow the argument to end.

Arguments Need to End

The baby self's most negative influence on arguments is that when failing to get its way, it cannot let go. The baby self in us has to convince our adversary to see it our way. We can't give up, we must keep trying—forever. Unfortunately, as an argument progresses, that effort becomes ever more frantic.

Let's say in the argument between Zack and Rita, Zack's baby self took control. Leaving would not have been an option. Instead, he would have had to pull out all the stops in order to change Rita's mind.

"No, we can't get a new couch, you just do not understand. We have to keep saving money. We're not moving ahead."

"I don't care about your obsession with moving ahead. I want a nice couch."

"But you have to care. You don't understand. Look, look! I'm going to get my bankbook. I want to show you what's been going on the last twelve months."

"I'm not going to look at your bankbook."

"What do you mean, you're not going to look at my bankbook? I just want to show you what's been going on. You have to look at it."

"I don't have to look at anything, Zack."

"But I have to show you what's been going on. You're being completely unreasonable."

"No, you're starting to get out of hand."

"*I'm* getting out of hand? *You're* the one who's out of hand. You won't even look at the bankbook. I'll read it to you."

"I'm not going to listen, Zack."

"But you have to."

The argument continues, but now it veers out of control. One or the other may say or do what he or she will later regret, something that could damage the relationship. Zack's baby self, its desperation now pushing through, tries to force its opinion on Rita. And Rita—her baby self provoked into action—retaliates in equal fashion.

It is normal in arguments for your baby self to get carried away with the arguing rather than let go and move on. But ultimately you need to recognize just who is running the show, and against the very strong feelings that it engenders in you—*No! No! Never!* screams your baby self—you must nonetheless let go. Despite its screaming, you must say what you have to say—but then end it.

The Value of Temporary Separation

In most arguments, only when the combatants are physically separated from each other can they calm down. Only when you are no longer engaged with that other person, now in a separate place, can the more rational voices within you begin to have their say.

She is a bitch. She really can be impossible. I really do hate her when she's like that, and she doesn't see what a bitch she can be. She never does.

BUT

Even though I won't take back anything I said, I can see where she's coming from. I can see how what I did must look to her.

So it was with Zack and Rita. They did end their argument. They did physically separate. Zack drives around in his car. Rita stalks around the apartment. They are mad. Now on their own, both have similar angry thoughts.

Rita: *He's such a baby. I don't need this. I could move in with my friend Lynnette, at least for a while. Let Zack worry about the apartment. I have money saved. My job's secure. I'll do fine. I don't need him. If I get my own place, I can play music as loud as I like.*

Zack: *Fuck her. I don't know if I can stand living with her for the next thirty years. I've seen apartment rentals in West River that are pretty cheap. It'd be more of a drive to work, but I could make it money-wise. Let Rita stay in the apartment. She can buy all the new couches she wants.*

But now separate, and with their angry feelings starting to wane, that other process starts to kick in. Even as Zack and Rita are picturing that separate future, a very different voice begins to surface—the voice of the mature self:

I really wish Zack weren't so uptight about money. We need to have a life. I want a house as much as he does, but I don't want to have to sacrifice everything just so we can put money away. The truth is that it's fine with me if he wants to get the fishing rod. I'm happy for him. He almost never spends anything on himself. But how dare he bitch at me about the place mats? And I do hate that couch. I think he has some kind of sentimental attachment to it because he saved it from his parents' garage when they were just about to throw it out.

And Zack, driving in his car: *I don't want to get a new couch. I know I shouldn't have said anything about the place mats, but it drives me crazy. I guess she's right that if I'm going to fuss about place mats, it's not fair for me to have gotten that fishing rod. And, yeah, she's probably right that I'm too crazed about sacrificing now for the future, but I can't help it. That's how I feel. But I do wish she would hold off about the damn couch. I know the old one's a piece of shit, but I like it, it has sentimental value. After all, I did save it from the junk heap.*

In the heat of an argument, it is impossible not to argue back, and it is very difficult to concede anything. Once Zack and Rita are apart, their thinking gradually becomes less one-sided. They won't necessarily change their minds, but in this now separated state they are at least receptive to the possibility. And maybe they *will* change.

Maybe a few weeks later, Zack will come to Rita.

"I've cut out sofa ads from the paper."

"You have?"

Or perhaps Rita might announce, "I don't know. I guess I can live with the couch a while longer. It is a lot of money. We can wait."

"We can?"

But maybe, as often happens, the issue never gets resolved. Maybe the question of getting a new couch, the conflicting opinions about spending money, will resume periodically. Arguments occur because there are issues about which the two parties genuinely do not agree. Some conflicts get resolved, but others remain as isolated pockets of continuing discord within the overall fabric of what may be a good relationship. It is not necessary that everything get worked out; it can't. What is necessary is that both partners acknowledge each other's feelings.

If we are not going to get a new couch, I want Zack to know full well that I hate the old one and will continue to hate it forever, and that he's just too cheap.

Rita might one day wear me down, but I really don't want a new couch.

Arguments do not have to be resolved, but it is necessary for each person to say his or her piece.

There is one last undeniable benefit of separating after ending an argument. Time and distance get to play their role. Often just the passage of time makes issues that had seemed so important then, issues about which you had felt so strongly, somehow seem less significant.

I cared a lot about it at the time. But now when I think about it, I don't seem to care that much at all.

Sometimes arguments achieve resolution, which is excellent.

"Give me six months and then I promise we'll get a new couch no matter what."

"If we can do it in six months, I don't see why we can't get a new couch now. But if that will make you happy, okay. But I'm marking it right here on the calendar in big red letters. See? May 27. New couch."

"I promise."

"I'm holding you to it."

But often they do not. What is most important for the overall health of a relationship is that each person feel that he or she has truly been heard. That is a primary need. Change comes, but usually it is gradual. And, of course, healing occurs with the simple passage of time. Baby self stubbornness gradually fades, leaving room for our more reasonable mature self, which can see where our real best interests lie.

It is not a requirement of a good argument that all matters be resolved. Plenty of arguments do not end with agreed-upon solutions. Often they end unresolved and not so agreeable.

"You are such a baby."

"Well, fuck you."

What is necessary with arguments is not that they resolve, but that they end.

Our Fear of Being Alone

Arguments can have two endings. In one, all is resolved and both parties go back to feeling good about each other. In the other, matters are not resolved, and if the argument has gotten heated, both parties are left with a residue of ill will toward each other.

I just discussed how it is often necessary that parties physically sepa-rate for the best outcome of an argument, as only then can time and rea-sonableness begin to have their beneficial effects. But as I explained earlier, the baby self must always feel fully connected to its basic source of love and security, and even the slightest disruption in the flow of per-fect connectedness is unacceptable. Baby selves, in their primitive reac-tion to everything, cannot understand that being mad now is not the same thing as being mad forever. Baby selves take the temporary discord of an argument and see its potential for the ultimate catastrophe: *The relation-ship might end.*

Being aware of this fact is key to avoiding the kinds of arguments with our closest family and friends that consistently get out of control. It is precisely the ability to conceive of the end of a relationship that permits arguments to conclude and facilitates the beginning of a far more mature process.

It is essential to be able to picture an alternate future in which you and the other person are no longer together. This is true for spouses, friends, relatives, and business associates. Why is this so important? Be-cause by being able to conceive of a separate existence, the mature self can neutralize the fear of being alone that so terrorizes the baby self. De-spite its screaming, separation does look at least possible.

"No, Baby Self, you are wrong. If Rita and I do end up separating, I will be very sad. I very much don't want that. But you are wrong. I will survive."

"Nooo! Nooo! Being alone. Nooo! We'll all die."

"No, Baby Self, we won't."

And once you are able to acknowledge that you *can* survive on your own, you can move forward. *Maybe we can work things out,* you'll tell yourself, *but maybe we can't. And maybe as a result, everything falls apart in our relationship. I would hate that. I desperately do not want that to happen. But it would not be the end of the world. I do have other options. I would survive.*

If you can conceive of a separate life, you can end an argument that does not resolve, you can walk away. This takes much of the desperation out of many arguments. And when we are not flooded by baby self terror, our more rational side has a much better chance to enter in.

The rules for communication that I have just described are pretty straight-forward. In an argument, you cannot solve everything. Everything does not have to get completely worked out, all loose ends neatly tied.

At some point, you need to let go. Sounds simple. It would be simple—were it not that our baby self is very clever. For in the furtherance of its primitive wants, as I said earlier, it tricks the more reasonable mature parts of you—and thereby slips by your more mature controls. You think that what you are doing is right and rational when it is anything but. Shortly, I will describe the baby self disguises that lead us astray. But first I need to talk about how the baby self—for all the trouble it causes—is not all bad. Not at all.

Part II

What Your Baby Self Says

Chapter 3

The Two Sides of Us

So far, I have been characterizing the baby self mainly as an enemy, a causer of problems. But as I said at the beginning of this book, the baby self is more good than bad. It is essential for our overall sense of well-being. It is just that often what it wants is not in your best interests. It is not evil so much as misguided. Viewing your baby self as an enemy is both inaccurate and not useful. It is on your side. Its primary goal is to have good stuff for you and no bad stuff. How wrong is that? But it is stupid. And it can be strong. Your mature self is good. But so is your baby self—it just isn't very mature.

What Baby Selves Like

Our baby self can be bossy and childish; it can lead us astray. But it can also be very good. It is at the center of our happiness. Switching into our baby self mode is how we nurture ourselves. It is our mode of refueling. It is the mode of stress relief. It is what we look forward to.

I am inordinately fond of food. Across the street from my office is a supermarket. Sometimes, just for a break, I go over to the supermarket and wander through the aisles, looking lovingly at all the wonderful food. I especially love the meat department.

Oh, look at those cube steaks.

I actually do this. Then, refreshed, I go back to my office and do some more work.

I have also been known between clients to play a game or two of solitaire on the computer. I can actually feel the stress flowing out of me as I sit there. Of course, sometimes it takes three or four games. Or five.

"Dr. Wolf, are you in there? . . . Hello!"

One great aid in getting through a rough stretch of work is the certain knowledge that there is going to be some pure baby self pleasure time in the not-too-distant future.

I have to complete this stupid job description by tomorrow afternoon. I hate it. I hate it. But Thursday I'm going to get veal parmesan takeout at Luigi's and rent Godfather: Part II.

It does help.

The baby self likes to

    Eat large quantities of butterscotch swirl double chocolate ice cream.

    Watch sitcom reruns.

    Play golf with friends.

    Take an afternoon nap.

    Do crossword puzzles (but not superhard ones).

    Watch a rental movie.

    Play fantasy league football.

    Have lunch with a good friend.

    Hear a stupid, very obscene joke.

    Make faces at somebody you love and have that person laugh.

    Play video games.

    Fall asleep on the couch while watching TV lying next to someone you love.

Have someone you love fall asleep next to you on the couch
   while you are watching TV (provided he or she doesn't
   snore).
Have any kind of physical closeness and touching.

And as I said, the baby self is at the center of all loving, nurturing relationships. It is how we can be ourselves. The baby self is the domain of
all that is impulsive and spontaneous. It sings. It dances. It makes silly
faces. It laughs. It has a sense of humor. There are certain people in my
life with whom I can allow myself at times to be totally me. Every so often
when I'm at work, I call one of them just so I can say something incredibly stupid that has come into my head that I think is funny. It is a brief
but major source of pleasure.

Pleasure Beyond the Baby Self

Our baby self supplies us with direct pleasure. But for a fully satisfying
life, we need something more. We need meaning. For that we need our
mature self.

Leonard spent his forty-seventh consecutive day watching rental movies
and playing video games.
   "How do you feel about yourself?" we ask.
   "I dunno. Okay, I guess."
   "Are you having a good time?"
   "Yeah, I guess."
   "Don't you get a little bored?"
   "I dunno. I guess. Maybe."

After a hard day at work, Albert spent the evening watching a rental
movie and then played a couple of video games.
   "How do you feel about yourself?" we ask.
   "Good. A little tired."

"Are you having a good time?"
"Yeah."
"Do you get a little bored?"
"No."

There is a different overall feeling about our life at any given moment depending on whether or not that life feels purposeful. A purposeful life feels deeper, more fulfilled. Living a life that lacks purpose makes us feel as if something were missing, no matter how much pleasure we are getting.

"No, it doesn't. I'm having a great time. Hey, babe, could you scratch a little lower, and while you're up, could you bring me another piña colada?"

"But don't you feel a certain emptiness, a certain lack of purpose in your life, a certain lack of inner meaning?"

"No. And while you're standing there, do you mind handing me that bowl of chips?"

But there *is* a difference. As humans grow, baby self nurturing alone cannot completely satisfy. Part of normal maturing is that baby self pleasure loses its ability to fully nourish the psyche. As adults, we require something more. We need to feel a sense of meaning and purpose in our lives. Feeding our baby self makes us feel good. But the feeling doesn't last. *We have to keep feeding it.*

"It was fun going shopping and having lunch out, but now I'm bored."

And though baby self feeding makes us feel good, it cannot touch that deeper place inside that can be fulfilled only through the mature self.

Meaning in life is exclusively the domain of the mature self. Meaning comes from two sources. One is striving to achieve a goal that is challenging and worthwhile.

Meaning can be very simple.

"I work to support my family."

"I take care of my kids."

Meaning can come from any goal that we decide is important to us.

This occurs when we throw ourselves into an activity, strive to do as well as we can, and extend ourselves to the fullest.

Lawrence studied the art of flower arrangement. He read everything ever written about flower arrangement. He went to Japan to learn from the masters. Finally, after twenty-two years of striving for perfection in the art of flower arrangement, Lawrence entered the floral arrangement world championships held every four years in Stockholm.

"And the grand prize, the Fleurs de Superb, goes to Lawrence Gallsworthy."

"Yes!" exclaimed Lawrence, falling to his knees and sobbing. "Yes!" as the powerful surge of triumph flowed through his body. "Yes!"

The true sense of purpose, of meaning, comes not in the final achievement, but in the process of having worked hard toward the goal. If success comes with little effort, it lacks the deeper satisfaction.

"And the grand prize, the Fleurs de Superb, goes to Roger Deckweather."

"Cool," said Roger, who on a whim had entered the contest that morning. "Yeah, I got this stuff I saw by the side of the road and put it together with my eyes closed. Cool."

It's not the same.

The other source of meaning for the mature self comes from being a valuable part of other people's lives—not just relating to them, but feeling that your relationship with them is important to them. Obviously, being a parent can supply this, but so too can being a friend.

Ben: "I really look forward to my Monday golf with Marty."

Jerry: "I really look forward to my Tuesday golf with Marty."

Carl: "I really look forward to my Wednesday golf with Marty."

It turns out that Marty has a golf buddy for every day of the week.

We ask Marty: "Do you feel that you fill any purpose?"

"Yeah. I'm a good friend. There are a lot of guys—I could name seven—who I know really look forward to our golf games."

Marty would not necessarily say this, but he would feel it. People care deeply about feeling at least a little bit needed. It gives them meaning.

What makes a full life? For that we need both our baby self and our mature self. We need day-to-day pleasure, but we also need a larger purpose.

Two Voices

There are always two voices inside of us—the baby self and the mature self. I depict them here mainly in conflict; more often they are not. Each has its place; both are part of what goes into making a full life.

At any given moment, we are neither all baby self nor all mature self. Both are there. But usually one or the other is dominant. For example, at work we're mainly mature self, but our baby self is there.

Hey, nobody'll notice if you check out the ads on eBay. This data revision is so boring. It'll be good for you to take a little break. You'll be more efficient. Come on. You don't have to be such a straight noodle all the time. Nobody'll know. No, maybe I better not.

At home, relaxed, well into our baby self mode, surfing the Web, we might allow the voice of the mature self to intrude: *I really should fix the toilet. I told Carla I would.*

The baby self swiftly responds: *Just a bit longer?*

Now, on its home turf, the baby self easily wins: *How about all afternoon? The toilet's not going anywhere.*

Tanya was invited for the first time to the home of a woman she had recently met.

"Can I offer you some ice cream? I don't know if you like butter cookie double fudge ripple"—which is, in fact, Tanya's favorite flavor in the world.

"Thank you, that would be nice, but just a little."

The mature self, firmly in charge, easily wins: *I don't want to seem too piggy in front of her. It would make a bad impression.*

But alone at home, the baby self rules.

Baby self: *This butter cookie double fudge ripple is so good.*

Mature self: *You disgusting pig, don't eat so much of it. You know you hate gaining weight.*

Baby self: *Look at the way the double fudge ripples through the butter cookie part. The ripples are so thick and chocolatey.*

After eating the whole quart, right from the container, the baby self is finally sated. Its desire is replaced by waves of nausea: *Oh, I don't feel so good.*

Now the baby self, its power diminished because it is no longer hungry, feels ill, and the mature self's voice comes back full force.

Mature self: *How could I have eaten the whole container? I'm so ashamed of myself. I'm a disgusting pig. What have I done?*

Waves of self-loathing flood Tanya's consciousness, her baby self having decided to take a nap.

Mature self: *How could you have done this to me?*

Baby self: *Urp.*

Both voices are there. Which voice dominates depends on the situation. The outside world tends to bring out the mature self. As I said before, being at home and with our nearest and dearest brings out our baby self.

But I'm So Tired

Ray and Eileen went to Eileen's mother's house for Thanksgiving. Before dinner, the guests and all of Eileen's relatives were sitting in the living room or the sunroom with drinks and appetizers.

"Ray, could you be a sweetheart and get me a drink of water with just one ice cube?" asked Caroline, Eileen's sister, who was seated next to Ray in the living room.

"Sure," said Ray, bouncing up immediately to get the drink for his sister-in-law.

After the meal, they were again back in the living room. Ray was now sitting next to Eileen.

"Ray, sweetheart, I'm feeling so stuffed. Would you be a darling and get me a Diet Coke with some ice in it?" asked Eileen.

Ray, who was very relaxed after the big meal, immediately felt a rush of resentment.

"I just finished a big meal, too. Why can't you get it yourself?" he hissed at his wife. "Oh, all right." Resentfully, he heaved himself out of his seat, feeling impossibly weighed down by his chore.

A few minutes later, Ray noticed that his mother-in-law, who had done a lot of the cooking, looked exhausted. He got up and went over to her.

"Kay, you look wiped out. Let me get you something. How about a Diet Coke with some ice in it?"

"Why, Ray, aren't you a sweet one. That would be really nice." Whistling to himself, Ray prepared the drink for his mother-in-law.

We interview Ray.

"Excuse me."

"Yeah?"

"We couldn't help noticing that you were very thoughtful about getting drinks for your sister-in-law and your mother-in-law, but it seemed to be a problem when it came to your wife."

"Yeah, well, I don't see why she couldn't have gotten it herself. I mean, I had just finished a huge meal, too. Why did she need to ask me?"

"But Eileen's asking you felt different from being asked by your sister-in-law and mother-in-law, didn't it?"

"Yeah, I guess so."

"Could you describe the difference?"

"I don't know, but whenever Eileen asks for something, actually whenever it comes to my doing anything for Eileen, it's different than for anybody else. It feels like a big chore, and I immediately resent that I'm supposed to do it. I don't know why it happens. It just does—automatically—whenever Eileen asks me to do anything."

Few of us are quite so honest with ourselves. Instead, we justify how we feel. We blame the other person, telling ourselves that the request was unfair:

It's the one time I really get to relax. I genuinely think Eileen has this thing where she has to ask me to do stuff whenever she sees me having a nice time, when I'm finally vegging out.

Our nearest and dearest, just by their presence, bring out the baby self in us. Hence, their requests often bring up immediate feelings of exhaustion and petulance, while the exact same requests from others to whom we are less close can inspire our generosity. It is not easy to rein in our baby self with those we love, but for the sake of being nice, it is always a good idea.

"Ray, be a sweetheart and get me a Diet Coke with some ice," says Eileen.

Great. I'm so stuffed. I can hardly move. I don't see why she can't get it herself. I'm really so exhausted.

But Ray only *thinks* all of the above. He says, "Sure, dear."

We cannot stop our baby self from surfacing. Fortunately, however, there is much we can do to ensure that it doesn't wreck everything.

Which Is the Real You?

If there are two voices, which one is the real you? Which one is how you really feel? Which one is what you *really* think?

Jellica was thirty-five, and her sister, Tremaine, was thirty-eight. They were both married, had children, and lived fifteen minutes away from each other in adjoining towns. Each year, Larry and Trudy Bernier, friends of both Jellica and Tremaine, had a New Year's Eve party. Their parties always had a lot of people and a lot of alcohol and always ended late. Neither Jellica nor Tremaine was a heavy drinker, but on this particular New Year's Eve, Jellica drank some, and Tremaine drank a lot.

It was one-thirty, and most of the guests were still there. Jellica found herself sitting next to Tremaine on the couch.

"You know what, Jellica?"

"What?"

"You're a stuck-up bitch."

"What?"

"You're a stuck-up bitch. Mom and Dad always favored you. I don't know why, but ever since I can remember I never could figure out how to get them to like me as much as you. And you always pretended not to notice it, but for my whole life you always put me down. Little things, but I notice. You think you're better than me, you always have. I don't think that you actually like me as much as feel sorry for me. 'Poor Tremaine, the best she could get was Alan.' I can hear it when you talk."

Jellica was stunned. She loved her sister and always thought they had a very good relationship. She had no idea Tremaine felt this way. Jellica was so shocked by the barrage that she didn't know what to say, so she didn't say anything.

The next day, she told the story to her husband, Scott.

"I feel terrible. I don't know what to say."

"Don't say anything," said Scott. "She was drunk, she didn't know what she was saying."

"But all those feelings. She didn't just make them up. They have to be there inside her. I can't believe she feels that way about me."

"She doesn't."

"Then where did all that come from? Why did she say it?"

Jellica continued to worry about it, but she didn't say anything to Tremaine. The next time Jellica talked with her sister—Tremaine had called to ask about a birthday party she was planning for one of her kids—Tremaine was very friendly, as usual. Neither of them brought up what had been said. It was as if it had never happened. It was not mentioned again.

Did I dream it? wondered Jellica.

What was going on?

We interview Tremaine and play for her a videotape of what she said at the New Year's Eve party. At first, Tremaine is shocked. She remembered vaguely that she had said something to Jellica, but she didn't remember exactly what. She thought it was probably no big deal. Jellica hadn't said anything afterward. Tremaine had no idea that she had said what she now hears on the tape.

"Do you feel that way?" we ask.

"No, I love Jellica. She's a good sister."

"Are you sure?"

"I don't know. I suppose that I have had thoughts like that at times. But I don't really believe them. I just think that sometimes Jellica maybe has said something, maybe not even on purpose, that was a little mean."

"Do you think what you said is true?"

"No, I don't think so. Omigod! Why didn't she say anything?"

"Are you sure you don't feel that way?"

"I don't know. Well, sometimes, yes. I guess. I love Jellica. She's a good sister. I don't know."

Did Tremaine mean all that she said to her sister at the New Year's Eve party? Were those her real feelings? Of course they were. Tremaine meant every word she said.

Our baby self is always with us. Our baby self picks up on all possible slights, feels jealous all the time, always feels taken advantage of, wants everything, and feels deeply injured when it does not get top billing. Tremaine meant every word, but what she said that New Year's Eve was only one opinion—that of her baby self. There was another opinion—her mature self's.

"Yes, I do feel that way, but the *majority* of the time I don't feel that way at all. I love Jellica."

Tremaine's mature self genuinely likes her sister, does believe that her sister likes her, knows that their parents loved them both, and does not feel that Jellica looks down on her.

Yes, on further reflection, thought Tremaine's mature self, *there is some truth to what I said when I was drunk. But* overall *I don't think that way at all. I do have those other thoughts, but just sometimes, in snatches. Yes, maybe Jellica can have that side to her. Occasionally she says some-thing that does make me feel a little hurt, offended. But* overall, *usually, no, she's nice. I love her.*

As a response to many situations, we often have more than one voice inside us. The baby self's voice is impulsive, reacts in the moment, makes huge generalizations from tiny instances, and is petty. The other voice, that of our mature self, is more reasoned, sees the big picture, and has a completely different perspective. But both voices are there.

It's called ambivalence.

Shawna is stupid. It was a mistake to marry someone so stupid. (Shawna did just say something pretty dumb.)

But actually I have a good marriage, and I almost always have a good time with Shawna.

———————

My life sucks. Nothing ever goes my way. (He's just been rejected by a woman he was trying to date.)

Actually, my life doesn't suck at all, but I have been on a recent losing streak with women.

I'm an idiot. I'm a fake. I really don't know what I'm doing. (She's just made a real mistake at work and had her project fail as a result.)

But I do seem to be successful at my job and, really, I think I'm pretty good at what I do.

I wish I'd never had kids. (It's the end of a snow day at home, when both kids were competing to see who could be brattier.)

No, I love my kids. I love having them—most of the time. It's just that on snow days I can seriously see the advantages of that nice 150-proof rum I used to drink sometimes in college.

I want to be free. I want to run where the wild wind blows. (She's just had an unusually tedious day at work, followed by disappointing pro-gramming on television that night.)

No, my life's okay. But maybe I should think about seeing Montana this summer. Or maybe it's Colorado in those ads I like.

What are you supposed to do about this other opinion inside of you that sometimes comes to the fore? Nothing. Recognize that the voice is there. Don't try to push it out of your head. You can't. Let the thoughts come, have their say. They may cause pain. But then they pass, and you can move on.

Every time I visit Eddie Palumbino at his house, I get jealous and I feel very dissatisfied with where I live. Then I start thinking about how I could have done a whole lot better than I did, and I feel very depressed about it. But it passes, actually pretty quickly. But when it's there, it's real and it makes me feel bad.

Ambivalence is a fact of life. We have more than one mind about the same thing. Often one of those minds belongs to our baby self. Its opinions, though often crude, are real. But more often than not, in a bigger context, a context that only our mature self can see, our baby self's opinion is not our dominant opinion.

The Baby Self Is Good

A guest at our holiday supper party gave us a box of very nice chocolates. The nicest of all were the ones with the hard toffee and fruit crème centers. After supper, Mary Alice opened the box and placed it out so that the chocolates would be shared by the guests.

Why should they get to eat the chocolates? They were a gift to me and Mary Alice. They'll probably go right for the ones with the hard toffee and the fruit crème centers.

I could feel myself getting upset. Unobtrusively, I moved over to the table whereon lay the box of chocolates. No one seemed to be watching. Carefully, I removed all the chocolates with the hard toffee and the fruit crème centers. Moving slowly, my hands in a position so that no one could see me holding six pieces of candy, I walked over to Mary Alice's desk.

"Is something wrong with your hands?" asked Mary Alice.

"No."

Otherwise unobserved, I dropped the six chocolates into a desk drawer. *They probably don't even like the hard toffee and the fruit crème ones. They probably would have eaten them just to be polite.*

With minor variations, this is a true story. Was I a bad person?

As I said, much of what I have written so far makes it seem that the baby self is a villain. But the baby self is not a villain at all; it is good, as long as it stays reasonably in its place. The baby self's domain is the world of fun. It is the baby self who can be silly, funny, extremely loving. The baby self loves to laugh.

The mature self tries but doesn't really get it.

"Do you want to hear a joke?"

"Sure."

"Did you know that *stop* spelled backward is *pots*?"

"That's a joke?"

"Yeah."

"It's not funny."

"Oh."

Without our baby self, we would be cut off from the most basic sources of pleasure in our lives. We would not be happy. Life would be flat and hard.

We all have a baby self. This means that as adults, all of us have thoughts and feelings that are selfish, piggy, jealous, bossy, maybe even downright cruel, and, above all, babyish.

I hate you.

I love you.

I want your cookies.

Look at me, not her.

I want to squeeze your arm and see if I can make marks on it.

No, I want it my way.

Across human history, there have always been people who have tried, through higher thoughts and discipline, not just to control their baby self urgings, but somehow to rise above them, to purify themselves so that their baby self was no longer a part of them—more accurately, to get rid of all the not-so-nice baby self urgings.

I shall purify my thoughts and the lowly urgings of my body, and I shall achieve a higher level of being.

The problem with this is that the baby self is not going anywhere. With the baby self, you get the whole package. You can't get just the love and the fun and none of the hate and pettiness. You can't get rid of the baby self—any of it. Some people try very hard to suppress their baby self: put it in a closet and stay pressed against the door. But since the baby self is all about wanting and caring, that caring gets pushed into the closet as well.

I have achieved perfection. There is nothing that I really want. I care about nothing. I have conquered desire.

Sounds like someone very depressed. No baby self, no joy in life.

I'm doing everything so well, I have achieved so much, how come I'm so miserable?

No matter how hard we try to repress the baby self parts of us, they remain anyway—a very real and continuing part of who we are. So what happens is we end up hating part of ourselves.

At one time, there was a lot written about "rediscovering one's inner child." Usually, this was directed at people who were depressed in their adult life, and the prescription for wellness was that they get back in touch with the child inside them. Often, those for whom this was most applicable had been parented with harshness. As a result, during their childhood they had been trained to repress the part of them that was normal and healthy, to see it as bad.

To have baby self wants and feelings—the good and the bad—is to be alive.

Fortunately, there is one major piece of good news about our nastier, not-so-helpful baby self urgings: We can think about doing something without actually doing it.

Maybe he would shut up if I squirted some of the ketchup on his shirt.

Her hair looks oily. I wonder if I reached over and touched it, would it actually feel oily?

We think these thoughts, but we don't act on them. Thinking about doing something and actually doing it are not the same. A universe lies in between.

With the extremely young, there is virtually no difference between intention and action; to think about it is to do it.

Yuck, these strained peas taste gross.

"Pfft!" and Baby Marvin spits the strained peas across the floor.

But as adults, having a feeling, having an impulse to do something, does not necessarily mean acting on that impulse.

Ugh, this pea soufflé tastes disgusting.

Herman chews and swallows it, smiling as he does so. But he leaves the rest untouched on his plate.

"Don't you like my pea soufflé?"

"It's delicious. I'm just really full. Really."

Many baby self thoughts, feelings, and impulses should not be acted upon. Yet those thoughts and feelings in and of themselves are not bad. Good and bad are what we do, not what we think about but don't do. Good and bad are about actions, not about thoughts.

I do not want to share my candy bar with Inez. I want it all for me. Besides, she's too fat. She doesn't need to eat half a candy bar. I'd be doing her a favor.

"Inez, would you like half my candy bar?"

"Yes, thank you, sweetie."

Damn. I really had wanted it all for myself.

"It really was delicious. Thank you. You're such a love."

It is not our thoughts, but what we do that matters.

Yet sometimes our more unpleasant, babyish impulses do get acted upon. Sometimes, ashamed to admit to ourselves that we have such babyish impulses, we believe our more palatable but incorrect rationalizations, unaware that we are unwittingly following the dictates of our baby self.

Chester: *I don't hate Helena* [his ex-wife], *and it's not that I want to get back at her and hurt her in any way I can. It's not that at all. I constantly question the kids about what goes on at her house and filed a lawsuit to get full custody because I really am concerned about the kids' best interests.*

He does not permit himself to see his own anger. Instead he thinks: *I don't hate her. I feel sorry for her.*

Not recognizing the anger, Chester has cut off his more mature side from having any control over these potentially hurtful impulses. He is free to act on the angry impulses because he does not recognize that they are there; hence he has no opportunity to control them with his more rational, more reasonable side.

Instead, we need to recognize the existence of our not-so-nice impulses.

I fucking hate her. I will always hate her. Any way I can make her suffer makes me happy.

With this admission, Chester is far less able to convince himself that his reason for going after the custody of his children is purely to act in their best interests. Admitting to himself that he really hates his ex-wife, he also becomes aware of that component in his motive for his pursuit of custody.

I want to hurt her where she cares. It is the one place I really can hurt her.

But now his conscience comes into play—and it may or may not control what he does.

It would give me great pleasure to know that the custody battle is making her suffer. But I know custody battles are not good for kids, and I don't even know if I want to win. I don't even know if it really is in the kids' best interests not to be with her.

And this is where the big advantage of not being ashamed, not condemning the unattractive parts, of our baby self comes in.

I know I shouldn't act on these feelings. But I'm not wrong, it's normal for me to feel this way. Of course I hate her. Who wouldn't? Who wouldn't like to see her suffer if he were me?

Chester ends up not going after custody, sparing himself—and his children—a lengthy and very unpleasant battle that he might not win anyway, and which he might not even have wanted to win.

When we refuse to recognize the baby self in us, we rationalize:

I want to do this because it is right.

We take it out of the realm of personal wants and feelings and put it into a false moral venue of right and wrong—where it does not belong.

Better:

I want to do this because I want to do this.

Recognizing and accepting the existence of our primitive, nasty, and immature baby self impulses and thoughts lets us step outside and see them for what they are rather than unknowingly acting them out.

Instead of:

Oh, that's a baby self motive. I don't think I really want to act on it.

We get:

No, it's not that I'm acting like a baby who wants only to get its way. Not that at all. Goodness, no. I do this because it clearly is the right thing to do.

Deluded into thinking that what we are doing is right, not recognizing it as an unhelpful baby self urging, we act—to everybody's detriment.

It is what I must do.

But it is not.

What If It Was Okay to Have a Baby Self?

What if having selfish, angry, very childish impulses in and of themselves was okay as long as you did not act on them? What if everybody had them? What if they were a sign that you were a regular human being with wants and needs just like everybody else?

As adults, we often feel ashamed of our baby self. We cannot help feeling that if others knew about, *really* knew about, our baby self side, they would look down on us.

"We used to have them over for dinner quite regularly. Really, they seemed like a nice couple. That was, of course, before we found out about *him*."

"Yeah, ever since my baby self side was exposed, the only place I can go, where I hang out every night, is the *Unsavory Person Bar and Grill*."

Almost all of us picture someone—a person we know, maybe somebody we know of, or maybe just someone we imagine—who exists on a far more mature, fully evolved level of being.

J. Helmsley Chatsworth—originally a highly respected lawyer for Chatsworth, Heming, and Landesman, and then judge in the federal court, a pillar of the community. His hobbies: chess and mountain climbing.

"I rose above my baby self a long time ago. You didn't? Oh, I'm sorry."

But what if baby self impulses were normal, not bad, and necessary for a happy life? What if baby self impulses were harmless as long as you didn't act on them? Mightn't they take on a rather different appearance?

When we go out to eat, Ingrid just goes on and on about herself. Sometimes it can get so irritating. And you know how when she talks she opens her mouth so wide? I really would love one day to stuff a napkin in it.

But what if you knew that though you might think about doing it, you never would? Mightn't the baby self urge even be funny?

What if we could say:

Yes, I have all these childish impulses, I do have this baby self side to me, but that's okay. I don't act on the really bad ones. They are, after all, part of being human. Everybody has them. Besides, without them I would be a lifeless robot. No spark. Joyless. No, as long as I can adequately control it, I like my baby self. It's actually funny how babyish my responses can be at times.

What if we felt this way about our baby self? Then maybe we wouldn't have to deny its existence so regularly.

The voice of the mature self helps us act better, and heeding that voice becomes much easier if our baby self is our friend. It is harder to be truly mature if, appalled at the baby inside of us, we try to deny its existence even as we act out its wishes.

Yes, I'm selfish. Yes, I get pissed off if I'm not getting my way. Yes, if I'm not getting my way, I don't seem able to let go, just leave it alone, accept it, and move on. Yes, I'm like that. But isn't everybody?

Why is it useful to see our baby self motives for what they are? If instead we believe only our high-sounding rationalizations, then we act with no second thoughts about our behavior. Our baby self runs the show while our mature self sits on the sidelines, duped into thinking itself a player when it is only a fool.

But if we see the baby self for what it is, we get to stand outside, look from a distance. The mature part of us comes back into the picture. We get to hear its voice.

Oh, that's the babyish part of me that wants to get its way. That's okay, I don't hate it, I like it. After all, I do like getting my way. But I know that's not always what's best. Maybe this time I'd better back off since last time when I didn't, it didn't work out so well.

Your baby self is your friend. It is, after all, you. But when it comes to your life and your relationships, your baby self is not always so smart.

Chapter 4

Because I'm Right

With any disagreements, the baby self side of us—the side that can never accept anything less than everything—can actually control our conscious thoughts. When we argue, ideas and convictions that we truly believe to be the thoughtful constructs of our evolved selves are not that at all. Instead, they are nothing more than the words supplied at the behest of that craving, mindless blob—our baby self—that won't let go because it's not getting its way. Some of what you—the mature you—think is the evolved and reasoned product of your emotional growth and experience is not that at all. You have been fooled by your baby self. It is a humbling concept: We are all not quite as mature as we think we are.

Of the justifications that we use for not letting go, none makes more trouble for us than *I'm right and you're wrong.*

In earliest childhood, when we do not get our way we cry and scream as long and as loudly as we can. As we develop language, we add words to our crying and screaming.

"I want it! I want it!"

"No! No!"

And, "Why? Why not?"

Then, as we get a little older and a little smarter and our verbal skills improve—we argue. We defend our point of view. And while arguing, we genuinely believe that we *are* right and the other person *is* wrong. But it is not even a matter of whether we actually are right. Our brain, as a direct descendant from earliest childhood, thinks, *I'm right,* and automatically brings up arguments to prove our case.

Celia and Louis had been invited to a dinner party at the Granik-Lambeaus' along with one other couple. Celia had accepted the invitation, but not before she checked with Louis.

"Sounds good," he had said.

Then, three days before the dinner party:

"Celia, you know the police picnic that Dad always goes to?" (Louis's father is a retired police officer.) "It's the same day as that Granik-Lambeau dinner party. He was going to go with his friend Patrick, but Patrick's not going, and Dad asked if I would go with him, and I said I would."

"You said what?"

"Dad asked me. Otherwise he has to go alone."

"You can't do that to me. We made a commitment to go to the Granik-Lambeaus'. It's too rude canceling at the last minute like this."

"Tell them that something unavoidable came up. Or you can go by yourself."

"I don't want to go by myself. It's too awkward, and it's embarrassing to cancel at the last minute. We don't know them that well."

"I already told Dad I would go with him."

"Well, you'll have to tell him you can't. It's too inconsiderate for you to back out at this point."

"I have a right to go with my dad if he wants me to."

"No, you already said that you would go with me. You have to tell your dad."

"No, I have a right to go. I don't want Dad to have to go to the police picnic by himself."

"Your dad knows tons of people. He can go by himself and do just fine. I'm your wife. You have to get your priorities straight."

"What do I care about the Granik-Lambeaus? I hardly know them. He's my dad. All you care about is making an impression on people we hardly know."

The argument continued, growing progressively more heated.

"How can you do this to me? You always do this. You are so inconsiderate."

"Me? You're the one who's inconsiderate."

But then a strange thing happened. Instead of being in their kitchen, Celia and Louis suddenly found themselves in what appeared to be a great courtroom. They were standing in front of an imposing person in judge's robes.

"I am the Ultimate Judge of Right and Wrong," said the imposing person.

"Oh, good," said Celia.

"Finally," said Louis.

And simultaneously they launched into their versions of the story.

"No, one at a time," said the Ultimate Judge of Right and Wrong. The judge then listened to both and gave his verdict.

Unfortunately, there is no judge. There is no absolute and clearly determined right or wrong. There are just two people—Celia and Louis—trying their best to work through a disagreement while keeping their overall relationship intact, not hating each other too much, and, at the same time, coming up with some kind of resolution that both can live with.

Does Louis have a right to cancel on his wife in order to accompany his father to the picnic? Or is Celia right that it is too inconsiderate of him to make her cancel at the last moment? Who's right?

The baby self never compromises, never sees the other side of the story. The baby self is dishonest. It never says, *I really, really want it this way. I really, really don't like it your way.* It says, *I'm right. You're wrong.* It is a way of bullying. All or nothing. My way or the highway.

And not only is the other person wrong, he or she is also a bad person. *Louis was wrong. He always does this. He is so inconsiderate.*

I'm not inconsiderate. Celia's the one who's inconsiderate. She always wants to get her way. And she always twists things around so that if what I want doesn't fit in with her plans, I somehow become the bad guy, when really it's just that she has to get everything her way.

A disagreement under the baby self's domination becomes two people heatedly criticizing each other:

"You're bad."

"No, *you're* bad."

What to do?

When you notice that you are engaged in a who's right and who's wrong battle, tell yourself the following:

This is not about right or wrong. This is about us wanting two different things. And we are not both going to get our way.

What I want and what you want allows for arguing, dealing, and negotiating. It is much more honest. When both participants recognize that they simply want different things, then and only then does the process of actual negotiation begin: *How much do I want it? How willing am I to take this loss? How much does the other person seem to want it? Is there any way I can compromise?*

This is the true basis of negotiation. We move away from petulance about moral imperatives to more empirical considerations. We start to weigh costs and benefits. Not right or wrong, but *What can I live with? What do I really care about? What do I maybe not care about quite as much?*

In the end, either we work something out or we don't. But either way, it's not about right and wrong or bad people.

She got her way and I didn't. She won this time. And maybe if, over time, I don't get enough my way, then maybe I don't want the relationship. But then again, because this time I didn't get my way, next time I'm going to try harder.

If both Louis and Celia had listened to their mature self and had known their argument was really about wanting different things, it might have taken a different course.

Notice what happens when Louis and Celia stay away from *you should, you have to, you can't do this to me, it's too inconsiderate,* and *I have a right to* and substitute *it's okay that we both want to get our way, but I really want to get my way.*

"I want you to go with me to the Granik-Lambeaus'. I'm embarrassed to cancel this late, and it's too awkward going alone."

"No, I really want to go with my dad to the picnic. I'm not comfortable with him having to go alone."

"He'll survive. He has friends there. And what about me? It's awkward canceling on them this late."

"It's not awkward. People do it all the time."

"No, it is *too* awkward. I don't want to have to cancel this late."

"No, I want to go with my dad. I don't want him to have to go to the picnic alone."

The difference between the two ways of arguing is subtle but significant. When right and wrong enter the argument, it becomes more personal; each participant feels under attack. Each feels more hurt, angrier, and hence more compelled to counterattack. But when the argument is simply two competing wants, a resolution becomes far more possible.

Maybe they will work out some kind of solution:

"I'll go by myself to the Granik-Lambeaus'. You go with your dad. But this really pisses me off."

Or, "Okay. I'll tell Dad I can't go with him because I already promised you. But he's going to be hurt."

Or maybe they won't:

"I'm going with Dad."

"But what am I supposed to do about the Granik-Lambeaus?"

"I don't know."

"I cannot believe how inconsiderate you are. I cannot believe it!"

But here the disagreement is about two individuals with conflicting wants, neither totally happy. What it is not is an official determination that the other is a bad person.

Following is a list of phrases that our baby self uses during an argument that leave us in an all-or-nothing position.

He's so wrong.

It's not fair to me.

I can't let her get away with doing this.

It's just not right.

I absolutely do not deserve this.

He always does this. It has to stop.

She's such a bitch.
He's such an asshole.
She's just like her mother.
He's just like his father.
She's a bad person.
How can he do this?

Obviously, the list is incomplete. You can no doubt add phrases of your own. When you are in a disagreement and notice your brain kicking in with any of these (or other) phrases, substitute:

I really want to get my way.

Let's take a look at another example.

Not so good:

"Come on, Jerry, let's go for a walk."

"I'm sorry, Janelle, I really don't feel like it."

"But you said you would."

"I'm sorry, but I just don't feel like it now."

"But you promised that you'd go for a walk with me."

"Yeah, well, I didn't know I'd feel like this now."

"But you can't do that. You told me that you'd go for the walk."

"Back when you asked me, I didn't know that when you finally got around to wanting to go on the walk I wouldn't feel like it anymore."

"I didn't *finally* get around to wanting to go on a walk. That was an hour ago. What did you think I meant?"

"Well, I guess I didn't think you'd wait this long."

"You're just trying to get around the fact that you promised and now you're backing down on your promise."

"I'm not backing down, you're being unreasonable."

"I'm unreasonable? You're the one who's breaking his word."

Who's right? Jerry certainly is breaking his word, but does he have a right to decline the walk now that he isn't in the mood? Of course, the question of who's right, who's wrong is what led to the problem.

Better:

"Come on, Jerry, let's go for a walk."

"I'm sorry, Janelle, I really don't feel like it."

"But you said you would."

"I'm sorry, but I just don't feel like it."

Now Janelle can go in either of two directions. She can, as she did, pursue the *you can't back down on a promise* issue—that is, Jerry is wrong not to want to go on a walk with her. Or she can focus on what she wants and how much she wants it.

"Please, Jerry. I really want you to come with me on the walk."

"I said I really don't feel like it."

"Please, Jerry."

Now the issue becomes something very different from what it was in the first example. It is now Janelle very much wanting Jerry to come on the walk with her and Jerry not wanting to go. Not *I'm right and you're wrong*, but *I want this and you want that*.

Maybe Jerry will relent, maybe he won't. And if not, Janelle may end up mad at him for disappointing her. But that's it. Jerry is not accused of being a bad person, and he has less reason to be angry, less need to get defensive. He may realize that he disappointed Janelle, which he did, and he probably will feel a little guilty, therefore predisposed to doing something nice in the future.

Our Phony Sense of Righteousness

Do not underestimate how skillfully our baby self can transform what is merely *I want* into what we truly believe are deep, important moral issues on which we must take a stand. So often where all we really want is to get our way, our baby self portrays our own selfish goals as something altogether different.

All day, Travis had been thinking about the spaghetti and clam sauce that he would have that evening when he and Ashley, his girlfriend of almost a year, had dinner at Carmine's Restaurant.

"No," said Ashley when he picked her up at her apartment after work. "Don't you remember you promised that we would go to The Good Earth, that new health food restaurant that I've wanted to try?"

"I'm sorry. I forgot. But couldn't we just for tonight go to Carmine's? I've been looking forward to it all day. We'll go to The Good Earth another time. I promise."

"No, I've been looking forward to going to The Good Earth all week."

"But I promise we'll go another time," said Travis, far from ready to give up on his spaghetti and clam sauce. "Tomorrow night we'll go, I promise."

"We can go to Carmine's tomorrow night."

"But please, you don't understand. I've been looking forward to Carmine's all day. I know it's stupid, but let's go this once, as a special favor."

"No, Travis, you promised. I want to go to The Good Earth tonight."

Travis could hear in Ashley's tone that she was not going to back down, and he *had* promised to go to The Good Earth.

At that moment, a red light went on at Baby Self Central. *Code red! Code red!* sounded a warning voice.

No spaghetti and clam sauce? sneered the baby self seated at the control panel in Travis's brain. *I don't think so.*

Deftly working the controls, the baby self moved into counterattack mode. *What to use? What to use? . . . Hmm. This should work.*

With a smile, the baby self pushed a button that read FEMINIST BULL-SHIT. Immediately the thought flashed through Travis's brain: *This is her feminist bullshit again. She never gives in to do nice stuff for me, because she thinks that if I ever get her to change her mind, she's not standing up for herself. Can't she ever simply be nice?* The thought filled Travis with righteous indignation.

"You know, Ashley, you can be really difficult sometimes."

"Difficult? I just want to go where you said we would."

"You're just doing this because you think that you're being taken advantage of anytime I ever get you to change your mind. Everything's some kind of fucking principle. Can't you sometimes just be nice?"

"What are you talking about?"

"You know what I'm talking about. You do this all the time."

"I do this all the time? All this is about is you wanting your spaghetti and clam sauce at Carmine's."

"See? That's what I'm talking about. Would it kill you just once to do a nice thing for me?"

"I can't believe you. You're unbelievable."

At that moment, we interview Travis.

"Do you really think that Ashley is holding firm about going to her restaurant because she genuinely wants to and you promised, or is she just being inflexible?"

"She's just being inflexible. She knows how much I look forward to certain meals once I have my heart set on them. I know she doesn't care that much about that place of hers and their zucchini casserole or whatever the hell they have. Everything's some kind of principle—not about us having an enjoyable time and having a good relationship, or about her once in a while doing something nice for me. Yes, that's what it's about."

If we hooked Travis up to a lie detector, it would show that he was telling the truth. He did believe that the problem was in Ashley. But it was not; it was all about spaghetti and clam sauce. Travis's baby self can make a convincing connection between Ashley's saying no and "feminist bull-shit." As long as an idea is believable, Travis's baby self latches on to it, thinks that it's true, and runs with it for all it's worth. The baby self takes the issue at hand out of the realm of personal disappointment and puts it into the altogether different arena of cosmic justice (*No, this is not me being disappointed at not getting what I want. This is something unjust, and the injustice must be rectified*) rather than the mature self way, which grieves and moves on: *I've tried, but I guess I won't be eating spaghetti and clam sauce. It's too bad. It makes me sad. It's a loss. But I guess I have to move on the best that I can. I hope I don't hate that Good Earth too much. Boo-hoo-hoo.*

A useful question to ask ourselves when in the middle of not getting our way is: *Is this just me not getting my way, or do I have a legitimate grievance?*

We may not know the answer, but just asking the question has a powerful effect, for it immediately allows us to step outside and create a distance between us and our baby self. The baby self only acts, it never reflects. Just the mental act of questioning our own behavior immediately calls forth our mature self and in doing so inhibits the impulsiveness that is our baby self. And often when the issue is really about our being piggy, just asking the question gives our mature self a much greater chance of controlling what we do:

"Oh, all right. We'll go to The Good Earth. But you have to promise we can go to Carmine's tomorrow."

"Yes, I promise. You're such a big baby."

"*You're* a big baby."

It is hard when we lose out on what we had been looking forward to; acting in a mature adult manner can be difficult. Our baby self will always go down screaming. But rising above the baby self is for the best if we want to have adult relationships.

No, it isn't. I want to go to Carmine's. Tell Ashley you just remembered that your doctor told you that you have a severe zucchini allergy and you'll probably die if you even set foot in The Good Earth.

Chapter 5

It's Not Fair

Fairness is the guiding principle whereby humans are able to live together in civilized societies. Fairness says that everyone by his or her birthright as a human being should get the same. It is a good principle and seems to work well as a means of resolving conflicts.

Our mature self, whose aim is to succeed and be accepted by others, buys into the principle of fairness as its guide for getting along in the world. Fairness becomes the main rule by which the mature self exerts control over the baby self. *You can't have everything, and you can't have everything your way; you can only have your fair share.* Our mature self uses the fairness principle to curb the baby self's wants so that it doesn't always wreck everything.

You won't get everything, but you will get your fair share.

But I want everything.

You can't have everything. That isn't fair. But you will get your fair share.

But I want everything.
No, you'll get only your fair share.
But I want everything.
No, only your fair share.
Oh, all right.
And the baby self retreats, grumbling, to its corner.
The baby self does not believe in fairness:
I'm supposed to give up stuff that I want? I don't get it.

Giving up anything "because it's only fair" is not something that the baby self ever does willingly. But the mature self, operating under the rules of fairness, has the power to control our baby self urgings.

But there is a hitch. For if our baby self can convince our moral mature self that what it, our totally selfish baby self, wants is our just due, what is only fair, then our baby self can slip by our mature self. Our mature self, sitting at the controls of our behavior, doesn't see our baby self's pigginess for what it is and allows it to pass.

You're sure this is fair?
Oh, yes, mature self. It's extremely fair (snicker, snicker).
Well, if you're sure that it's the fair thing to do, I guess it's all right. You're sure now?
Yeah. Yeah. I'm sure.
Well, okay.

ONE LOBSTER PER CUSTOMER read the sign over the all-you-can-eat seafood bar.

"Hey, look, there's a guy, I saw him. That's his second lobster. And none of the restaurant workers said anything. That's not right. Why should I take only one? Why should I take only two?"

"George, that's your sixth lobster."

"What's your point?"

That is, there is another fairness. The baby self's fairness.

A great many years ago, in a secret chamber deep inside the bowels of Mount Morensco, the Grand Baby Self met with its councillors.

"We need something," said the Grand Baby Self. "I fear that the forces of the mature self may now slowly be gaining the upper hand. Our 'never let go' campaign has done well, as did our 'everything is not enough.' Though 'moving on is for sissies' was a little less successful. We definitely need something, or I fear the worst."

Much discussion followed, but it produced nothing particularly new. Then Cute as a Puppy Baby Self, one of the quietest (and hence least respected) of the baby self's councillors, spoke up.

"I have an idea."

"Yeah, right," sneered the others.

Cute as a Puppy Baby Self persisted. "Fairness. My idea is fairness."

"That's a stupid idea, and you're stupid," scoffed the other baby selves. "That is one of the mature self's deals, and we hate it. It's where you have to give up stuff because 'it's only fair.' "

But then Cute as a Puppy explained his idea, and the beauty of it brought a hushed silence from the gathered councillors.

"We'll have our fairness," said Cute as a Puppy Baby Self, "only it will be about getting instead of giving. We will fool the adult world and the mature self. Our fairness will use the same rules as, will have the same name as, the mature self's fairness—except it will be only about getting."

As one, the councillors rose to their feet, the chamber exploding with their applause and cheers.

"Teach it to all the baby selves," shouted the Grand Baby Self.

The rest is history.

Early on, children perceive that the idea of fairness is one to which adults seem to give much respect. Early on, the baby self learns that "It's not fair" seems to have far greater success at getting what it wants than yelling. And not only does the baby self say, *It's not fair*, it learns to generate examples and arguments that demonstrate how truly unfair it is. And not only does the baby self create all these corroborating arguments and evidence, it also brings up an accompanying sense of great outrage.

The baby self—who believes whatever it says because it said it—fully believes in its great sense of injustice.

Rather than *I'm not getting my way, and that makes me mad and frustrated,* our baby self learns to say: *This isn't fair. This isn't right. I deserve to get my way.*

And the mature self is fooled:

Well, if you say it's not fair—and your arguments do sound convincing—then I guess I will let you do what you want.

The baby self latches on to the concept of fairness as a powerful tool for getting stuff from the world. The baby self in adult life constantly scans its environment, looking for anything that might be out of line. And if it perceives even the slightest imbalance, the baby self jumps on it for all it's worth. As long as the imbalance remains, the baby self will hang on, fixated on the perceived unfairness, endlessly.

Our Endless List of Grievances

On the way back from the beach, Kimberly wanted to stop at the factory outlet stores. She told Bryant that it wouldn't take long, and since it was right on the way and she really wanted to, she didn't think it would be a big problem. Bryant, who had no interest whatsoever in the factory outlets, waited in the car. Thirty-five minutes later, Kimberly returned. They drove home.

About fifteen minutes from their house, Bryant asked, "Is it okay if I stop at Plant and Garden? I want to pick up a couple of bags of mulch."

"I'd really rather not. They are so slow." (Which was true.)

"It will take ten minutes, fifteen at most."

"Can't you some other time? I'm tired. We've had a long day. I'm sorry. I just want to go home."

"But it was okay for you to stop at the factory outlets?"

"Bryant, I'm tired."

"I'll be ten minutes. No more."

"Bryant, I want to go home."

"It's not fair, Kimberly."

"Bryant, I want to go home."

They went home.

The rest of the way back to the house, and in fact for the rest of the evening, Bryant kept bringing it up.

"It's okay when you want something. But anytime it's for me, there's always some reason why not."

"Bryant, will you please drop it?"

"But it's not fair. You get what you want, but I want to stop for ten minutes, and no, you're too tired. It's always okay for you, but never for me."

"Bryant, that's not true. I do things that you want. What about the time you wanted to stop at Video World last week?"

"Yeah, that was once. Besides, I was getting a present for Errol. No, it's always about you, never me. You want examples? I'll give you examples. What about last Saturday in the supermarket? It was fine to get the more expensive coffee that you like, but when I wanted to get the lamb chops, no, it cost too much."

"Bryant, that's not the same."

"Oh, yes, it is. It's always for you, but not for me. And what about the curtains?"

"Bryant . . ."

But now Bryant's brain was in full gear as it began to supply him instance after instance in which Kimberly had gotten things her way and he hadn't. And with each example, his outrage grew.

"What about the time at your father's with the toaster? Hunh . . . what about that?"

Bryant sulked. Kimberly was mad at Bryant for carrying on so much. It ruined their evening. In fact, Bryant was not so mad about not being able to go to Plant and Garden. It was the unfairness that bothered him.

We all have a mental ledger. On one side is a list of everything—*everything*—that the other person ever did, didn't do, got, or didn't get. The money he spent for a new updated DVD player when the old one still worked fine. The time he accidentally broke the can opener. The time she sulked in the restaurant when he ordered more coffee and she wanted to leave. The time she didn't get the flu when he did. It is a list of specific past instances of unfairness from which can be pulled any or all items that might prove useful at that moment to make your case. It is the baby self's ledger. Of course, the ledger has only one side. On one side is everything that might be to your advantage. On the other side of that ledger, where one might expect to have the bad things that you did and the good things that you got, there is nothing. The other side of the baby self's ledger is a complete blank.

"What about the time you lost your temper at me because we got stuck in a long supermarket line?"

Not on the baby self's ledger.

"What about the time you got all that special attention after your knee operation?"

Not there.

Bryant was right. It was unfair. He was not wrong to tell Kimberly that he thought it was unfair that she would not agree to let him stop at the garden store. As discussed, he tells Kimberly what he thinks and how he feels. Kimberly hears him. But the baby self does not stop there.

We talk to Bryant.

"You say I should tell her that I think she is unfair and that's it? But that's not enough. I have to get her to see how unfair she is. It's not fair. Kimberly always gets to do stuff her way, and when I want something for me, she always gives me a hard time."

"Do you think you could get her to see it your way?"

"No, I have already tried. She doesn't see it at all, and she is not going to. That's the problem."

"So what are your choices?"

"You just want me to forget it and move on. But I can't. It's too un-fair."

Our baby self grabs us by our esophagus and screams, *No, it's not right! It can't stay this way.*

At the least, we want recognition.

"Hey, Randy. It's Bryant."

"What's up?"

"I just want to hear your opinion. I'm going to tell you the story and you tell me what you think."

"You and Kimberly, hunh?"

Bryant told the story of stopping at the outlet stores and not stopping at the garden store.

"Boy, that's not fair."

"You really think so?"

"Yeah."

"I knew it."

But usually we can't get even that. And really, our baby self wants more.

What does Bryant actually want? What will actually satisfy Bryant's baby self?

"Okay, I'm going to show you. I have videotapes of everything that has ever gone on between me and Kimberly. A panel of impartial judges chosen by both me and Kimberly has watched all the videotapes. They have given a weighted score of from 1 to 10 for each instance of unfairness either on my side or on Kimberly's side. The total unfairness scores were then added up. They have just calculated the final results. Here they are.

"I knew it. It came out plus 1,462 unfairness points on my side. I knew it."

"Now, what are you going to get for all your unfairness points?"

"Isn't that obvious? From now on I get to have 1,462 points' worth of things between me and Kimberly to my advantage until all the points are used up."

"Kimberly, do you agree to this?" we asked incredulously.

"Yes, now that it has been shown to me with mathematical proof, of course I will. It is only fair."

We ask Bryant.

"Are you satisfied now?"

"Yeah, this is the way it is supposed to be."

The problem is that in real life our baby self is going to be constantly frustrated. For every unfairness it wants a payoff. But the mature self has a saying, "For each instance of true unfairness, that plus $1.50 will get you a cup of coffee." What you get as compensation for unfairness is nothing. And when you pursue the injustice past your initial statement of unhappiness, you invariably only make matters worse.

Yet if we move past these instances of unfairness, don't get too hung up on them, a funny thing happens: The passage of time makes them far less relevant.

Actually, overall I like my relationship with Kimberly. She drives me crazy sometimes. And, yes, I think it is unfair that she wouldn't stop for me to get the mulch. It's just that now it doesn't really bother me. Right now I can't seem to get too worked up about it, because overall I'm happy with our relationship. I know it was unfair. But right now I don't seem to care about it like I did then. I'm not really sure why I felt it was such a big issue.

In the end, standing issues of unfairness rarely resolve. More commonly they wax and wane in our consciousness. But in the long run, the bigger picture prevails.

Is there some way we can counter our raging and dispel the stomach-binding feeling that such gross unfairness must be dealt with? Is there some way we can tap into the awareness that seems to come only later, when we get some distance from the moment—the saner realization that it was not at all the big deal it seemed to be at the time?

It is what I said before: What you get in recompense for all the unfairness is nothing. That is the one piece of information most relevant to the baby self within us. It allows us to move on.

I want her to know about the unfairness, but what I am actually going to get is nothing.

Only this knowledge can stop you from the self-defeating pursuit of yet another example of unfairness.

In any long-term relationship, there are constant inequalities. Some of the inequalities are a real problem for us. But others, we do not care about at all. However, the baby self, who screams at anything out of balance, will always make a giant problem out of any unfairness. Under its influence, we lose sight of the more important reality: Overall, the relationship is fine.

Fairness is always an aim, but if your goal is actually to resolve a conflict, ask yourself these relevant questions: "How much do I really care about it?" "How much do they really care about it?" Within a relationship, there is a guide far more useful than strict fairness as a working basis for resolution. That guide is: *what works best for the both of us.*

"It's Okay If You ... but If I ..."

Every evening between eight and nine o'clock, Edward, who had a high-pressure job, liked to read the newspaper or some magazines. It was his "quiet reading time." But sometimes Dylan, his partner of many years, wanted to talk.

"What do you want to do Friday night?"

"Dylan, please!"

"Do you think we should make plans?"

"We can talk about this later. Please, just let me have my quiet time."

About fifteen minutes later, the phone rang. It was Stefan, one of Edward's colleagues at work, calling to chat. Edward put down his paper and chatted happily with Stefan for an hour.

Later, Dylan confronted Edward. "It's okay for you to talk on the phone to Stefan during your sacred 'quiet reading time,' but you have a fit if I try to talk to you except if the house is on fire or something."

"I don't understand your problem. You know my quiet time is very important to me."

"Yeah? So how come during your quiet time you can talk to Stefan?"

"I don't see your point."

"It's okay to talk to Stefan, but not to me."

"Stefan called on the phone."

"You could have called him back."

"Why would I want to? What is your problem, Dylan?"

"The problem is that you're being completely unfair to me."

Edward doesn't see it and never will. Dylan is left stewing at the unfairness.

It's not fair. He has a fit if I try to talk to him during his stupid quiet time. But it's fine if he wants to talk to friends on the phone.

Dylan is right. Edward's rule for his quiet time is inconsistent, and Dylan gets the short end of the deal. Dylan bridles at the unfairness. At the least, he wants some recognition from Edward. *I could live with Edward's unfairness if he acknowledged it.* But Dylan's not going to get that satisfaction. It is here that Dylan's baby self could make unnecessary trouble. Under its influence, Dylan could get hung up on the unfairness and lose sight of an important point: He has never really minded granting Edward his quiet time. Occasionally, he finds it frustrating when he wants to talk to Edward. But the quiet time itself has never been a problem for Dylan.

Under the influence of his baby self, Dylan might have kept trying to get Edward to see his unreasonableness, which Edward won't and which would only create a more serious argument. Or, Dylan could retaliate. *I'll show him!* Dylan could intentionally bother Edward during his quiet time or set up his own quiet time just to show Edward "how it feels," a quiet time that heretofore Dylan had never had any interest in.

But in this case, Dylan chose to follow another alternative preferable to strict fairness. He chose the *How much do I actually care? Does it work for me?* route. Two relevant facts: Dylan has never minded the quiet time, and Edward can be blindly self-centered. This latter fact Dylan has always known. Long ago, Dylan had come to terms with that flaw in Edward, because overall he, Dylan, liked the relationship anyway. So in this case, Dylan let Edward know he was mad.

"Edward, you really are a jerk. You are so unfair, and you just don't see it."

But after getting frustrated from his attempt to open Edward's eyes, Dylan dropped it. He moved on.

The story continues. A month later, Dylan rented a movie, the intense four-hour epic *The Sun and the Shadow.* Dylan had already seen it twice and loved it. He wanted to watch it again and really get into it. He wanted to see it uninterrupted—without any disturbances.

Two hours into the movie, Edward came into the room with some tools and started banging at a window latch.

"What the hell are you doing?"

"I'm fixing the window. It will take me five minutes. I'll put the movie on pause if you want."

"What are you talking about? I'm watching the movie. I don't believe you're doing this. You know that it's *The Sun and the Shadow.*"

"I just have to do this one thing. It will take me five minutes. You can't pause the movie for five minutes?"

"Edward, get out of here! Do it later. I'm watching the movie."

"Jeez, what's your problem?" said Edward as he left the room.

Dylan finished watching the movie in peace but later made a point of speaking to Edward.

"What the hell were you doing? You knew I wanted to watch the movie. You have a fit if I say anything during your precious quiet reading time."

"This is completely different. That's just an hour and it's during the week after I have a hard workday. You know that. This has nothing to do with that."

"Yes, it totally does. I don't ask for a whole lot. But the one time I want to watch a four-hour movie, you can't deal with it."

"It's not the same thing and you know it. I'm not allowed into the room for four hours? Will it kill you to take a five-minute break? You're such a prima donna."

"I don't believe you."

"I don't believe *you*."

Again, Dylan fumed to himself. *He can have his time when I am not even supposed to talk to him, and the one time I don't want him to talk to me, he makes fucking house repairs. And if I try to get him to understand how crazy and how unfair that is, he just does not get it.*

Again Dylan is right. Edward was being an inconsiderate jerk. But Dylan told Edward and made him leave. End of story. Or perhaps, as Dylan did, he can bring it up again later on if he is still mad.

"You are an inconsiderate jerk."

Still, Dylan's baby self screams for more: *It's unfair. I have to get him to see the unfairness.* But Dylan has to move on. Listening to that voice and making Edward's unreasonableness part of the bigger issue of fairness only leads to frustration and resentment on both sides.

The story goes further. Dylan, who worked for an advertising agency, rarely brought home work, but he had a presentation coming up on Thursday and needed to work on it at home Wednesday night. Tuesday night—after quiet time, of course—he spoke to Edward.

"Tomorrow I'm going to need the living room all evening so that I can spread out all my stuff to work on my Thursday presentation."

"I have to stay out of the living room the whole night?" Their big TV was in the living room. There were two other perfectly good, but smaller, TVs in other rooms.

"Why can't you do it at the library? They have big tables."

"What?"

"Why can't you do it at the library? They have big tables there."

"What?"

"What's wrong with the library? It's five minutes away."

"Edward, you are the most selfish, self-centered person in the entire world."

"I'm supposed to sacrifice my evening when you have a perfectly good alternative?"

"I don't believe you. You expect me to give you your quiet time every day, but God forbid I ask you for something I need to do for work—to be a little inconvenienced—and you have a fit."

"I'm not having a fit. And I don't see why you can't go to the library. It's not fair to me."

"Not fair to you? This is my house, too. I'm allowed to work here."

"But you can do it somewhere else, and I wouldn't have to be a prisoner in the bedroom all evening with the little TV."

Again, Dylan should view Edward's behavior in the overall context of their relationship. Edward can be impossibly self-centered. Dylan knows that. But he can also be very generous and considerate; he is basically a good and caring person. Edward is always solicitous of Dylan when he is sick or sad, a good listener, very giving of time and money, and a kind person. Dylan is happy with the relationship. But Edward is also at times blindly selfish.

Overall the relationship works for me. Edward does have his maddening blindness, but overall the relationship works for me.

Dylan is happy with Edward. There really is not a problem.

Dylan can try to cure Edward of his unfairness, but that crusade will never succeed. Dylan must move on. Within a relationship, there are other issues that transcend absolute fairness:

What I really care about. What I don't care about that much. What I can live with. What I can't. What works for me. What works for us.

A Sample List of Grievances

We all have our baby self ledgers. Below is a sample list. Make your own list, but be warned, your blood pressure may go up in the process.

He never turns out the lights, but he always makes a big fuss about throwing away money on heat whenever I forget to close the front door even if I am bringing in groceries.

She leaves her dirty clothes on the bedroom floor but has a fit if I ever just leave dishes in the sink.

He eats stuff out of the refrigerator that I bought especially for myself, but if I dare to touch any treats that he buys for himself without first asking him, he goes ballistic.

When he has a problem I am a good listener, and I will always give him as much time as he wants. But whenever I come to him with something I need to talk about, he is always impatient and can't wait for me to finish.

I always laugh at her jokes, but she usually makes a face like "What kind of person would ever think that was funny?" whenever I tell a joke to her.

She will talk to friends about personal stuff between me and her, but she gets real upset if I ever do it.

He will never let me say anything critical of his mother, but he often says derogatory stuff about my relatives.

If we have an argument, she thinks nothing of trying to bring the kids in on her side. But I try never to do it because I think it is wrong.

I am willing to see movies with him that I am not really
interested in seeing, but he'll never do that for me.

She is allowed to be critical of me but gets all bent out of shape
and hurt and offended if I ever say anything negative about
her.

In restaurants, he'll sit forever drinking coffee after a meal
even if we have a movie to make. But at home, he bolts
from the table as soon as we finish eating to go in and
watch TV.

It is part of human nature to notice each and every annoying thing
our partner does, every inconsistency. We are not wrong to have such lists.
But it is damaging to a relationship to bring them up constantly; we must
move on!

"I Never Would Have Done That"

Unfairness within a relationship always gives us trouble, but certain im-
balances bear specific mention, as they are particularly hard for us to get
past. We all know the saying "Do unto others as you would have others do
unto you."

But what if you do unto others and the others don't do the same
unto you?

———

Derek and Malcolm were going to the Charlie Griffin concert that Friday
night. Malcolm had picked up the tickets to the sold-out concert, and
Derek was going to repay him. But Wednesday evening, Malcolm called
Derek.

"Hey, Derek."

"What's up?"

"I just found out my cousin Lonnie is going to be in town over the
weekend. I hardly ever get to see him, and the only night we can hang out

together is Friday night. So I'm going to go with him to the concert. Sorry if I screwed up your plans, but Lonnie and I go way back, and like I said, I hardly ever get to see him. Listen, I'll give you a call and maybe we can do something next weekend."

"Well, screw you," said Derek, and hung up.

What's his problem? thought a puzzled Malcolm.

Derek was mad. *Yeah, right. I'm really going to make plans with him next weekend. I can't believe he did this to me.*

Derek called Malcolm back. "I can't believe you. We made plans."

"I'm sorry, Derek, but I told you, my cousin Lonnie is going to be in over the weekend and I never get to see him. You and I can do stuff together anytime. I'm sorry you're pissed."

"I can't believe you. I never would have canceled plans we already made in order to go with somebody else."

"Well, that's your problem, isn't it," said Malcolm.

"Well, screw you again," said Derek, hanging up again.

I never would have done that to him. That's so inconsiderate.

The more Derek thought about it, the madder he got.

I would never have done that to him.

It was true. In the same situation, Derek would have felt that it was unfair to Malcolm to cancel on him. Derek either would not have spent Friday night with his cousin or he would have offered both tickets to Malcolm, sacrificing his going to the concert.

Fuck him, fumed Derek, getting mad all over again when he thought about it. *I never would have done that to him.*

We are especially vulnerable to being hurt when others act toward us in ways that we genuinely would not have acted toward them. Our baby self is not about to let that pass.

Not get something in return for good behavior? Excuse me.

How would he like it? thought Derek. *I would like Malcolm to see how it feels.*

"I can arrange that."

"Who are you?"

"I'm the author of the book you're in."

"I'm in a book? Cool. Can you change my face a little and give me better abs?"

"No. That's not what this book is about. But I can make Malcolm see what it would be like if the shoe was on the other foot."

"Yeah, I want to see that."

Now it is Derek's cousin who arrives on the scene.

"Hey, Malcolm, it's Derek. I'm not going to go with you Friday night. I'm going with my cousin Chuckie, who's coming into town."

"Oh, shit. I really wanted to go to the concert."

"Well, sorry."

The conversation ended.

"Now, Derek, we're going to interview Malcolm to see how he feels when he is on the other end of the deal."

"Malcolm, what did you think about Derek's shooting you down for Friday night?"

"I don't know, he wanted to go with his cousin."

"Aren't you angry?"

"Yeah, I was pissed because I was looking forward to it."

"Aren't you mad at Derek?"

"I don't know. He wanted to go with his cousin."

"But don't you think it was inconsiderate—in fact, really rude—of him to cancel on you, shut you out at the last minute like that?"

"I don't know. He wanted to go with his cousin."

"Well, it was inconsiderate," Derek said later. "Malcolm just doesn't see it. I wouldn't have done it to him."

What to do?

Demanding that others act by the same principles as you only leads to hurt and disappointment. What works better is to act well. If you always expect rewards for your good behavior, and regularly feel hurt when others don't reciprocate according to the same rules, you are acting well, but with strings attached—which really isn't such a nice way to act.

As always, there is a mature self take on the story.

I do this because it is how I choose to act, not because I get rewarded for my behavior. I would like others to act toward me as I act toward them, but I can't expect it. Maybe I'm a fool, and maybe I'm letting the world take advantage of me. But it's my choice. I can act this way or not. But I cannot expect that others will act as I do.

For Derek, this translates to *I would never do that to Malcolm, but he's not me. I act as I do because that's me. But Malcolm's not me. I can hope, but I can't expect that Malcolm will act as I do.*

The rule: *Do unto others as you would have others do unto you. But do so because you choose to, not because of what you'll get in return. It's your choice.*

Still, the baby self does have a point. If we followed the Golden Rule and never got anything positive in return, it would be very tough. Fortunately, if you consistently act well toward others, you generally have a nicer life. People like you. The more selfish alternative, *I'm going to be considerate of others only when they do the same with me,* makes for a perennial chip on your shoulder and is a much more unfriendly way of going through life. If you act well, generously, and considerately, people will like you. Not everybody will like you all the time, but a whole lot more will than if you followed the alternative: *I won't do for you unless you do for me.*

And of course, if people disappoint you regularly, you don't have to have anything to do with them.

Let's look at another example.

"Hi, Leslie, it's Tisha. I know it's last minute, but could you take Richie and Jackie this morning for a few hours? I have a hair appointment, and then I need to look at sofas at Wildinger's. I was going to drop them off at my mom's, but she has a headache. It will be only three or four hours, tops. Do be a doll. I'll be over in fifteen minutes. Thanks a bunch."

I can't believe her, thought Leslie as she subsequently spent her morning running around her house looking after Jarren and Todd (her two kids) and Richie and Jackie. *I would never ask somebody that much of a favor. Who does Tisha think she is?* Leslie fussed the full four and three-quarter hours that Richie and Jackie were at her house.

"It was a big success," Tisha said when she finally picked up her children. "Don't you think my hair looks great? And you would love this couch I saw, it's maybe a little formal, but I love it. Jackie and Richie, go out to the car before Mommy starts getting mad."

Leslie fumed on. *I would never impose on somebody like that.*

Leslie would never impose on somebody like that. But Tisha would. She is Tisha. Others don't live by the standards that we set for ourselves. They have their own.

What should you do when others don't act by your standards? Say to yourself: *I can keep acting as I have or not. That's my choice. But others are not necessarily going to act as I do—because they are not me.*

She Doesn't Do Her Share

We get mad when others don't operate by our standards. This can be a big problem when it comes to sharing a workload. We may have one sense of what's right, while they have another. It may seem that they are not holding up their end of the responsibilities, but they may look at it from a completely different perspective.

Evelyn and her sister, Isabel, both lived about twenty minutes away from Whispering Oaks Nursing Home, where their eighty-one-year-old mother had been living for the past two years since her stroke. Both Evelyn and Isabel led comparably busy lives.

"Thomas," Evelyn said to her husband one night, "I'm worried about the evening shift at Whispering Oaks. They've taken on two new girls since Mrs. Crawford and that nice Judy left, and I really don't think they're checking up on Mother the way they should."

"I'm sure they'll be fine. The others will teach them."

"I'm not so sure. I think tomorrow when I go over there, I'll—nicely— chat a little with those two new girls."

Evelyn did have the chat and felt better. She had always believed that establishing a good relationship with the staff at the home got better attention for her mother. Evelyn visited Monday, Wednesday, and Friday afternoons and Sunday mornings. Her visits usually lasted a couple of hours.

Isabel went over to Whispering Oaks twice a week, on Tuesday nights and Saturday mornings. She stayed for about an hour. Evelyn had never been comfortable with how much less time Isabel spent visiting their mother, but she had never said anything. But now Evelyn continued to worry about Thursday afternoons. She had spoken to the afternoon workers, but she remained uneasy.

When I am there visiting Mother, I see some of the other residents. Many of them just sit around. Nobody pays any attention to them. Maybe they're watching TV, but really they are not doing anything. I feel bad about Mother on Thursdays.

Finally, she spoke to Isabel. "I feel bad about Thursday afternoons. I don't think anybody pays attention to Mother at all. I picture her just sitting there. I was hoping that maybe you could go over, even for just a short visit, on Thursdays. I think that it would make a big difference to Mother."

"I really can't, Evelyn. Thursday just doesn't work for me."

"Well, maybe we can switch days around. With work I can't get over there more than three days. I know that it would be an extra afternoon for you, but you must be able to work something out."

"I visit Mother twice a week. I think that's enough."

"I don't see that it's asking so much. She is our mother. I have always taken a major responsibility for making sure she's okay. Now I'm asking you to do a little bit more because I can't do it all."

"I know you do more than me, but nobody's asking you to do it."

"Mother needs us."

"Evelyn, it's a good nursing home. I'm happy for all you do. But I think Mother is fine."

"She's not fine. She had a stroke."

"You know what I mean."

"You don't want to do any more because you don't want to be bothered. I thank God that I'm around, because I don't know what would happen to Mother."

"Evelyn, that's not fair."

"No, you're the one who's not fair."

Isabel did not visit Thursdays. A chill developed in the sisters' relationship.

I can't believe how selfish Isabel is. She's always been like that. All she thinks about is herself. And she's ready to take advantage of me if it will save her any inconvenience.

Again, the baby self cannot let it pass. *She's not doing her fair share.* But life presents circumstances in which our level of commitment and caring, our judgment of what needs to be done, exceeds that of the others involved. They just don't see it the same way we do, and we are left doing more and feeling taken advantage of. The real problem—again—is that we want others to be like us. It does not work.

Isabel is not Evelyn. She sees it differently.

I care about Mother as much as Evelyn, but I just don't seem to worry about Mother being at Whispering Oaks the way Evelyn does. I don't feel the need, and I am not willing to put in the same kind of time as her. I'm happy that Evelyn does as much as she does. But I just don't feel the same about it.

Evelyn's outrage gets in the way of her seeing the real issue and dealing with it.

Isabel is comfortable with a lot less involvement with Mother and her care at Whispering Oaks than I am.

The baby self screams, *It's not fair! I have to do something about it.*

The mature self reasons, *Other people aren't me, and I can't expect them to be.*

If others do not hold up their part of a job, try to get them to do more. But if that doesn't work, then you have a choice. You can continue doing as much as you have been doing, or you can do less. Those are your choices. At that point, fussing is not a really good option.

Here's another example:

After seven years as an attorney at Witherspoon, Chapin, and Fitzgerald, Jennifer was leaving the firm to start her own practice. Anthony, Jennifer's best friend at the office, suggested to their co-workers that they give Jennifer a good-bye party. They agreed. Anthony was very gung ho about the idea and mapped out an elaborate plan for the following Friday from noon to two. The others seemed okay with Anthony's plan, but as the time drew nearer, it was Anthony who was doing most of the arranging. And though he griped to his co-workers, nobody did much to contribute.

"If you hate doing all this work," said Charlie, "why don't we just have potato chips with sour cream–onion dip and Kool-Aid?"

"Jennifer's been here seven years. How would you feel: seven years, and they have potato chips and Kool-Aid at your good-bye party?"

"I'd feel good. I like potato chips and Kool-Aid."

On the morning just before the scheduled party, his co-workers still not helping, Anthony blew up.

"You're all lazy, self-centered bastards," he shouted, running down to his car and coming back with a very large box containing 260 buffalo wings, which he plunked down on the floor in the middle of the office. "I can't believe all of you. Sure, let Anthony do it all. He's a sucker. I don't care what you do. I'm done with it." He stormed out.

But his co-workers weren't taking advantage of Anthony. They just weren't as interested in the party as he was. Anthony liked the idea of the party—it was his idea to begin with. He liked doing the work for the party. So what was his problem? Once Anthony's baby self, ever vigilant for unfairness, picked up on the fact that there was unequal participation, it made him lose sight of his enjoyment of the project. He got hung up on the perceived unfairness and ruined everything.

Baby self: *If it's unfair, I have to do something about it.*

Mature self: *If I'm happy with it, who cares whether it's unfair or not?*

Holding Grudges

There is one particular use of the balance scale that is consistently destructive in relationships. This is the idea that for every transgression there must be a balancing negative consequence meted out intentionally to the transgressor. In the legal system, it is called justice. But within the realm of human relationships, it all too easily turns into payback and revenge.

In a relationship, when we are hurt by another we have two competing and simultaneous instincts. On the one hand is the mature part of us that wants to do what is best for the relationship—to keep it going, despite the hurt, in as positive a direction as possible. The other urge—pure baby self—is retaliation. Having the desire to retaliate is normal, but acting on it is invariably destructive; revenge in response to hurt is always a mistake. But when wronged, our baby self, in order to get past our mature self, invariably invokes the name of justice. The baby self says to us:

> *I can't just let her get away with this.*
> *I have to teach him a lesson.*
> *If I don't do something bad to her in return, how will she ever*
>   *learn?*
> *He deserves it.*
> *It is only right.*

Never underestimate our ability to delude ourselves into thinking that our motives for revenge are pure. Sadly, the baby self's version of justice invariably sets off the terrible downward spiral of injury for injury.

.

"Hi, Bernadette, it's me," said her husband, Joe. "I need you to do me a favor. I was going to take my gray suit to the cleaners on the way to work, but I forgot. I need it for that meeting on Friday, and if I take it in tomorrow, they won't have it ready in time. Would you mind?"

"Joe, you know it's my day off. I was just going to hang out and maybe go over to Mother's around noon."

"But I really need the suit. The cleaners is only fifteen minutes away."

"I don't want to promise."

"But I really need the suit for Friday."

"I guess."

"Thanks."

As the day developed, Bernadette did not feel like driving to the cleaners.

That suit's okay. I saw it when Joe last wore it. It will be fine. It doesn't have to go to the cleaners.

"Did you remember to take my suit to the cleaners?" asked Joe as soon as he got home that night.

"No, I didn't feel like it. It's my day off. The suit's fine."

"No, it's not. I told you I really need it for Friday."

"The suit's fine. I saw it."

"Thanks a lot, Bernadette. Thanks a whole lot."

Joe checked out the suit, decided it looked slightly rumpled but would have to do. Still, he was mad. He really wanted to look his best for the meeting.

"Where were you?" demanded Bernadette the next evening. "Don't you remember? You promised you'd leave work a little early and be here for the kids so I could take that special double aerobics class."

"No, I remembered, but I had a lot of stuff to do."

"But you promised you would be home early. I missed most of the class."

"Yeah, well, I'm sorry. I had a lot of work to do," said Joe, not sounding sorry at all.

"You're still fussing because I didn't take your suit to the cleaners."

"Yeah, well, you didn't, did you."

That Saturday, Bernadette went shopping with her friend Simone.

"Don't forget I have a tennis date with Buzz at three-thirty," Joe called out as she left.

"Yeah, yeah."

Bernadette and Simone were having a good time. They shopped, stopped for latte and hazelnut biscotti, and shopped some more.

"I thought you had to get back by three-fifteen," said Simone.

"Yeah, but I'm having fun with you. Joe plays tennis with Buzz twice a week. It won't kill him to miss one time," said Bernadette.

We appear.

"This is just what Joe did to you earlier this week," we say.

"No, it's not. He was acting like a jerk. He wore the suit, it was no big deal. I don't see why I should give up a really good time for him since he was so petty and made me miss my aerobics class."

"Where the hell were you?" Joe asked when Bernadette got home.

"I was having fun with Simone."

"I missed my tennis. Buzz was really pissed."

"He'll survive. The two of you play tennis twice a week."

"Well, fuck you."

The next morning, Joe was going out to Quick and Ready to pick up the Sunday paper.

"Joe, would you take my car and fill it with gas while you're out?"

"Fill it yourself."

That night, Joe was taking a bath when Bernadette came in to get a Band-Aid.

"Could you hand me that towel?" asked Joe, who was starting to get out of the tub.

"Why should I?" said Bernadette, and walked out of the bathroom.

Again we appear. We ask Joe, "Don't you think you're both acting like babies?"

"She is, but I'm not. If Bernadette is going to act like she's acting, why should I do anything extra for her?"

We go out and ask Bernadette.

"Bernadette, don't you think you're just coming down to Joe's level?"

"No, he's acting like a baby. Why should he expect me to do him any favors?"

"But aren't you doing exactly what he is doing?"

"No. He's the one who decided to act like a jerk. As long as he's acting that way, why should I do anything for him? It's not fair to me: doing for him and him not doing for me."

Here's the same story with a twist.

Bernadette was in the store with Simone, looking at tablecloths, when Bernadette looked at her watch and realized that she would have to leave soon if she wanted to get home in time for Joe's tennis date.

No, I don't think I'm going to. I'm going to stay here with Simone. Why should I give up my good time for him? Why should I be considerate after he screwed me over about my aerobics class? After all, it's only fair.

But let's say at that moment the voice of Bernadette's mature self kicked in.

I want to stay here, and after all, Joe acted like a jerk. But maybe it's better if I get back to being nice to him. He doesn't deserve it. Still, I know it will be better if I act nicely even if I don't feel like it. One of us is going to have to start being nice, and I guess I shouldn't be a baby about it.

But Bernadette's baby self was not about to just lie down and die.

No, he made me miss my aerobics class. Why should I also miss out on having a nice time so that he can play tennis with Buzz? Why should I have to? That isn't fair to me.

In effect: *It's okay if I act like a baby because it's only fair.*

But in this instance, Bernadette's mature self prevailed.

It really is nice for everybody to be nice. I want to be nice. That's what I want from my relationship with Joe—for us to be nice to and considerate of each other. But aren't I freed from having to be nice because he wasn't nice? I don't know, I suppose I should go home.

"I'm home."

"Love you," said Joe as he headed out the door for his tennis game, relieved that Bernadette was not still mad at him and even feeling a brief flash of tenderness toward his wife now that they were back on good terms.

In this example, there are two paths to two alternate universes. In one universe, Joe and Bernadette enter into a negative, unending cycle of meanness and retaliation. In the other, they move on, and the result is positive. It's obvious which universe is better. Yet standing in the way of entering the far more pleasant universe is the baby self's justice, not letting him or her get away with it, making the other person pay for what he or she did.

Deep inside of us all is an intuitive sense that bad acts cannot go unpunished. *It's not right.* Justice has its place, but where justice is at the expense of kindness, consideration, what works best for everybody, *that* justice is neither more nor less than a tool of the baby self going after its pound of flesh.

Chapter 6

Not So Useful Responses to Misfortune

I have said earlier that when you don't like what has happened in a relationship, it is best to say what you have to say and then move on. But at the heart of why this is so difficult for us is the baby self's response when any unpleasantness comes into its life. This applies with all that is unpleasant, from the smallest personal slights to genuine tragedies—anything at all that creates bad feelings. Obviously, you want to get as much distance as possible from all that is bad. If something bad happens, you want to get it behind you. But unpleasant occurrences—from the smallest to the largest—are something the baby self can never move past.

Bad Is Not Good

The baby self will never just let bad feelings happen—it has to actively do something to change them. So it resorts to either (or both) of two basic strategies to make the bad feelings go away. It may, as just discussed, seek revenge against the wrongdoer, or it may try to get something good as recompense for the bad. To cancel out the bad feelings, the baby self wants something in return.

Think about it. We have all been raised in a culture that encourages this. The United States is famous for having far more lawyers per capita than any other country in the world. This vast army of lawyers results from the idea that if something bad happens to you: *Quick, call a lawyer.* Maybe you can get a bunch of money. Early in life our kids learn the words "I'll sue you." Physical injury is great ammunition for revenge, but if you can add on mental suffering as well—better still!

For the baby self, it starts early in life.

For anything bad, I have to get something good.

Innocent versions of this:

You hurt my feelings. I want a hug.

I had a bad day at school. I want ice cream.

Somewhat less innocent versions:

You were mean to me yesterday. I want a present.

I've had these headaches. I should be the one who gets the seat in the restaurant with the best view of the water.

Unfortunately, some people develop a particularly pernicious variant. Not only does bad deserve good, bad *is* good. Bad is good because it can get good stuff. This is not a conscious process. They genuinely do feel bad. They do deeply believe they're suffering. But the baby self inside sees the injury as a potential source of getting good stuff. And obviously, the greater the degree of injury, the better the chance for a bigger, better reward. As a result, the suffering becomes exaggerated, extended. Bad things that happen are to be held on to, cherished, for they are a way of getting good in return.

As the mature self knows, bad is bad. We want bad to end. While this concept may sound simple, the competing voice of the baby self can get us very confused. Underneath what feels like hurt can be the less obvious motive of looking for benefits.

Elsa and Oliver were longtime friends of Beverly and Charles Toricelli. Their kids had been in Pee Wee Soccer. They occasionally went out together, sometimes invited each other over, and both spouses had regular contact with their same-sex counterpart. They were not best friends, but they were good friends.

Jessica, Beverly and Charles's eldest daughter, got married. Jessica and Rocky (her fiancé) wanted a small wedding. Relatives were invited, along with friends of the bride and groom and a *few* close family friends. Beverly and Charles invited the Millers, the Wrenvilles, Daniel and Hope Westerman, and Richard Crandall. That was it. Elsa and Oliver were not invited.

"The Westermans?" said Elsa. "I can understand the Millers and the Wrenvilles, and I suppose Dick Crandall. But the Westermans? Beverly didn't meet Hope until four years ago. We've known Beverly and Charles for ten years. I mean, I like the Westermans, but that's not the point. I don't get it. We're closer to Beverly and Charles than the Westermans are."

"I don't know," said Oliver. "Maybe they're sucking up to the Westermans because they're rich. Daniel's store has to be really pulling in the bucks."

"We're not good enough for them?" said Elsa. "I thought we were good friends. Not good enough, I guess."

A month later, Charles Toricelli called Elsa and Oliver. He asked Oliver if they were doing anything Saturday night and if they wanted to go out to dinner, something they had done many times in the past. Oliver said he would get back to Charles.

"I don't know," said Elsa. "I think they have a lot of nerve, not inviting us to the wedding and then acting as if nothing happened. If we're not good enough to get invited to the wedding, we're supposed to fall all over them when they want to go out with us to dinner?"

"Yeah," agreed Oliver. "I don't think I want to be their second-class friends."

Oliver and Elsa decided not to go. A coldness developed between the two couples, and over the next few months their friendship dissolved.

Until Jessica's wedding, the couples had been good friends. After the wedding, because Elsa and Oliver had not been invited, they were no longer friends.

In this situation, where does the baby self's thinking that bad is good fit in? What can Oliver or Elsa possibly get from holding on to the snub and thereby ending the friendship? It certainly seems like a loss. What were they after? It is the aim of the sulker. Part of Oliver and Elsa's reaction was, of course, to get back at Charles and Beverly.

We'll show them.

But there was another, deeper piece. Not just revenge, but—against all logic—the feeling that somehow by holding on to the hurt, they will gain something. We can all at times embrace the feeling of hurt. We speak of wallowing in self-pity. We hold on to the sense of being wronged, as if somehow there is something right about it.

What can possibly be good about feeling bad? It is, of course, our baby self, who will use anything if it thinks it can get something. What do we want? Something. Anything. What did Jim want? What did Elsa want? Let's ask.

"What do you want, Elsa?"

"I don't want anything. I just feel hurt."

"What about if you were told—you name the price—that you could get compensation from the Hurtness Judge?"

"That's silly."

"How hurt are you? Give me a figure."

"Stop it. This is ridiculous. It's an insult."

"Any figure. What's a fair price for your hurt?"

"Stop this. I'm leaving."

"How about a hundred thousand dollars? I'm writing the check. All you have to do is cash it. I'm putting the check down on this table and I'm leaving."

Later the same day, Elsa spoke to Oliver.

"What do you think?"

"A hundred thousand dollars is a lot of money. We could really use it. What do we have to do?"

"Not be mad at Beverly and Charles anymore."

"How can taking the money change that?"

"I don't know. Do you want to do the deal?"

"Yeah, sure."

A number of months later:

"I'm glad we didn't get invited to Jessica's wedding, aren't you?" asked Elsa.

"Yes," said Oliver as they sat by their new in-ground swimming pool.

"Do you feel mad at Charles and Beverly?" asked Elsa.

"No, not at all, honey."

"Me neither."

There is another, more useful response to personal hurt than always trying to get something in return. That response is to feel bad. To take the bad—*they hurt our feelings*—for what it is, a loss. To feel sad. To grieve. But then to move on.

We feel hurt that Beverly and Charles did not invite us to the wedding. Hurt that we aren't as high on their list of friends as we thought we were. We don't feel as good about Beverly and Charles as we did. It's sad. It's a loss.

But then when Beverly and Charles call to invite them out to dinner, Elsa and Oliver might have a different reaction.

They apparently still like us. They want to continue the relationship. I don't feel the same way I used to about them. But they still seem to want to be friends. Let's see how it goes.

And maybe there will be a different ending to the story.

"Elsa, Charles Toricelli just called. They want to go out with us Saturday night. What do you think?"

"I don't know. I still feel hurt about the wedding, and apparently they just don't see it. But I guess it will be all right. What do you want to do?"

"Well, maybe we're their second choice to the Westermans, but we always have had a good time with them. Let's say yes and see what happens."

The two couples go out and have a good time. They remain friends. The snub of Jessica's wedding is always there in the back of Oliver's and Elsa's minds. They do not forget it. But as time goes on and the friendship continues to the mutual enjoyment of both couples, the snub feels a whole lot less relevant.

Elsa and Oliver were not wrong to feel hurt for not being invited to the wedding. They were not wrong to feel angry at the snub. Bad is bad. But it is something to get past, feel sad about, and then let go of. However, not so the baby self. It wants something in return. And because there isn't really a Hurtness Judge who goes around giving recompense for wedding snubs, if we heed the voice of the baby self, all we get is more bad.

Holding On to Hurt

"My name is Jeremy. I am afflicted with the tragic psychological disorder HESS: hyperemotional sensitivity syndrome. Those like myself burdened with this terrible disorder are doomed to suffer more than others. What to you, a normal person, may be small slights, light emotional taps that you can easily shrug off, are like sledgehammers to us, emotionally shattering, crushing us, causing terrible, lasting damage to our extraordinarily delicate psyches. . . .

"What? Why are you looking at me that way?"

"What way? I wasn't looking at you any way."

"Oh, God, now you're mad at me, too. I suffer so much. Really, I have to lie down."

"You're a nutcase."

"See, nobody ever understands. My pain, my suffering."

The tragic case of Jeremy may be a bit extreme, but there is no question that people—to varying degrees—can devote their lives to suffering.

Emotional hurt is real. Suffering is very real. But the baby self, always looking for the possibility of getting something good, has a way of taking very real hurt and running with it for all it is worth. In doing so, it can destroy relationships.

"What's that, Chad?"

"That's a picture of me and my four college buddies, Robby, Wally, JJ, and Benson."

"You guys look pretty happy."

"Yeah, we always called ourselves the Five Musketeers. We did a lot of stuff together, let me tell you. The Five Musketeers, we were quite a crew."

"Do you still see them?"

"Well, actually, no. I don't have contact with any of them."

"Why not?"

"Because people disappoint you, that's why not."

"Tell me about it."

Chad did. He told a story of how each friend had hurt him in a way that he could not forgive.

The time Robby, who lived in another part of the country, had come to town for four days and hadn't even called Chad, who learned about the visit just by chance. "How could he do that to me if we're supposed to be such good friends?" (Robby had thought about calling Chad but was in town seeing relatives and chose to spend the whole time with them.)

The time Wally had completely ignored him at a barbecue, preferring to talk to some of his buddies from work. "I felt so insulted." (Wally had spent the whole evening talking with his work friends. It hadn't even occurred to him that Chad would mind, since he saw Chad regularly.)

The time he and JJ had been talking and JJ said that he always had thought Chad was selfish. "How could he ever say something like that to me? I was so hurt." (The conversation had not been a deeply serious one. JJ was just saying what he thought was a fact and didn't think that Chad would feel hurt.)

The time Benson had chosen not to schedule their regular tennis hour anymore because he wanted to play with another guy who was a better tennis player. "Did our friendship mean so little to him that he could abandon me like that? I was so hurt." (It was true. Benson wanted to get better. He knew Chad would probably feel bad about it but assumed he would just find somebody else to play with.)

"So you're just a lonely, bitter guy now?"

"No, not at all. It's just that people disappoint you. Besides, I've got Rusty. Come here, boy. See how he loves getting his ears rubbed. Good boy, Rusty."

Under our baby self's supervision, the hurt that would normally diminish with time does not diminish at all.

Debra and Douglas were a couple. Though they enjoyed each other's company, Debra repeatedly got into snits over insensitive things that Douglas said, and she would stay mad at him. Douglas, who was basically a good-hearted guy, sometimes made such comments. For example, one time Debra didn't properly close the door to the refrigerator. Some food spoiled and had to be thrown out. In response to this small tragedy, Douglas had said to Debra, "How could you be so stupid?"

It was an insensitive and unacceptable thing for Douglas to have said. In response, Debra got mad.

"What did you say?"

"I'm sorry."

"Don't you ever call me stupid."

"I'm sorry. That was wrong."

But as regularly happened, Debra was not mollified. She remained in a snit for the rest of the day.

"You need to understand how much what you said hurt me."

But according to Debra, Douglas never got it. And this she berated him about continuously.

Debra's real hurt, and she's real mad at me. I know sometimes I say stupid stuff. But Debra makes such a big deal out of it. She's always mad at me over something I said. I try not to do it. But I don't think what I say is so terrible. But no way can I get her to see that. It only makes her more angry.

Douglas got tired of the snits, tired of always being in the doghouse over something. He broke up with Debra.

Any relationship, especially a close long-term relationship, is going to include good and bad. Obviously, you want to emphasize the good and minimize the bad. When the bad occurs, express your displeasure, share what you are feeling, and make it clear that you do not want it to happen again. But that's it. Holding on to hurt is very human, but it also is self-defeating and debilitating for relationships.

But I want them to know how I feel.

Letting others know when they have hurt you is important. If those close to you do not understand how you feel, especially if you have strong feelings about how they hurt you, a gap can develop. Because your feelings are such an integral part of who you are, when they aren't acknowledged, an important part of you is lost from the relationship and to that extent diminishes the relationship.

How can you let others know that they have hurt you, even when they don't seem to get it? How do you know if your reaction is too much? By all means, tell them, let them know. But then move on. How can you make sure they get it, that they really understand? You can't. One of the hard parts of being mature is that there's a lot of uncertainty. Moving on often means not working everything out.

There is a big difference between *I want them to understand* and *I want to make* sure *that they understand.* You can make a lot of trouble if you try too hard to make them understand how you suffer.

What to do?

When you have been hurt and want others to know about it, tell them. But if you are still letting them know, you need to ask yourself some questions early on:

What do I want? What more do I want? Am I actually going to get anything more? Is this really useful?

You need to recognize emotional hurt and give it its due. But there comes a point when that hurt no longer serves any useful purpose. Though a part of you may want to hang on to it, you have to say to yourself, *That's enough. Stop.* It's hard to do, but in the end—as always—it makes for a nicer life.

Taking Losses—Two Universes

Whether we choose to hold on to hurt or not can make a profound difference in our lives. If we suffer a true loss, we need to accept the hurt caused by this loss—because we have no other choice—but then we have to move on. Only moving on can save us from a path of self-destruction.

Mariel was driving through an intersection, the green light in her favor, when some teenagers, speeding, failed to stop in time at the red light and rammed into her car. Mariel sustained serious injuries that left her with neurological weakness in her left leg. She was told that she might have to walk with a cane for the rest of her life.

The three teenagers suffered injuries, too, but none were serious. It turned out that the seventeen-year-old driver, Darron Dexter, was from a wealthy family. Mariel sued for damages, and Darron's father's insurance company quickly offered a substantial settlement. Mariel's lawyer told Mariel that she might be able to get more if they went to court, but also she could get less. He advised her to accept the settlement. Mariel fussed over it for a week before accepting it. Immediately, however, she worried that maybe she had made a mistake. Maybe she should have held out for more.

Meanwhile, Mariel was slowly regaining strength in her leg. She was in a rehab program, but the process was slow and the rehab arduous, sometimes painful. Mariel was not as diligent about going to her rehab sessions as she might have been. Also, somehow, she kept seeing Darron Dexter—at the mall, getting out of his new car at a gas station, coming out of a haircutting salon.

Why does he get such a carefree life? (Darron had gotten two citations for speeding and for going through a red light but had not lost his license.) *He gets a new car, and I'm permanently crippled. Why did this happen to me? I didn't do anything wrong. I should have tried to get more money.*

Then, at a party, Mariel found herself talking to a lawyer. The conversation turned to her accident.

"How much did they settle for, if you don't mind my asking?"

Mariel told him.

"Oh," said the lawyer. "I'll bet the insurance company was happy with that. You could have gotten a lot more."

Mariel consulted another lawyer. "I want to reopen my case."

The lawyer said that because she had agreed to the settlement, the case was closed. Mariel tried to sue the Dexter family directly. *Maybe their insurance rates went up for a while, but this has basically cost them nothing.* But again she was told that she had accepted the settlement and that was it.

Over the next few years, Mariel consulted six different lawyers but got nowhere.

Mariel now walked with a noticeable limp. She no longer participated in sports, which she used to enjoy. Although Mariel's doctors told her that if she continued her rehab there might still be some improvement, she saw little change. *What's the point?* she felt, and discontinued rehab.

Four years after the accident, Mariel was so despondent that she ended up on antidepressant medication, which helped some. But she was still pretty miserable.

The combination of a bad car accident and the baby self made a mess of Mariel's life. Her reactions were all extremely normal. All of us would have felt the unfairness of her situation, been bothered by Darron Dexter's nice life, and worried that we had settled too quickly. But not everybody's baby self—fussing endlessly about a closed case—would have dominated so thoroughly.

In an alternate universe, another version of Mariel reacted differently to the same initial catastrophe. Four years later:

"It's four years and you still walk with a limp."

"Yeah, I probably always will. But I have a nice life. There's still a lot I can do, and I hate to admit it, but the settlement changed my life. I'm not rich, but with the settlement, money is not the big worry it used to be."

"Don't you worry that you could have gotten more?"

"Sometimes I think about it. But once you settle, that's it. So what's the point of fussing about it? Like I said, the money I got has made a real difference in my life."

"What about Darron Dexter? You must see him sometimes. Don't you feel resentful?"

"I did. But what's the point? He was just a kid. That's what kids do—drive recklessly. I had the bad luck to be in the wrong place at the wrong time. To be honest, I really don't think about it much anymore one way or the other."

"What about your limp?"

"What can I do? I worked at rehab the best I could. This is what I got. I walk. I get to places just as easily. And I've taken up swimming. Sometimes I feel sad remembering what I used to be able to do before the accident. But to be honest, I really don't think about this a lot. Sometimes I think about the limp, but I get past it. What choice do I have?"

These two stories are both possible outcomes for the same happenstance. The only difference is that in the first, the baby self—with its inability to let go—ruled.

Sadly, bad is bad—whether it is not going to a restaurant we want, a crippling car accident, a watch that we lost in a movie theater, or a partner we love and have no plans to leave but who at times says hurtful things. Bad is bad. We need to get past it, not dwell on it.

If we find ourselves fighting to fix genuine bad that cannot be undone, we again need to ask the questions:

Is this me unwilling to accept that the bad really has happened, or is there genuinely a point to my pursuit? Can I undo the harm that's been done?

The baby self and the mature self have two completely different reactions when bad enters their lives. The mature self first tries to change it and then, failing that, tries to get as much distance—time and space—as possible from the bad. But not the baby self.

Picture a soda machine in the middle of a desert that takes coins but gives nothing in return. After the mature self puts in its coins and gets nothing back, it might kick and bang the machine a few times, but if it still gets no results, it moves on. But the baby self will stay by the soda machine forever, kicking and banging.

Chapter 7

It Always Has to Be
Somebody's Fault

The baby self's response to everything is primitive. Not only can it not move past bad, but bad always has to be somebody's fault. The ubiquitous bumper sticker of some years back, SHIT HAPPENS, would be incomprehensible to our baby selves. The baby self literally cannot understand that a bad event could just happen. Its world is very limited, very small, and very simple—*me and you now*. And if bad enters the scene, someone *has* to be blamed. This is a problem, because not everything that goes wrong is somebody's fault.

The French Club at Northvale Regional High School was going to France. Emily Trezblidian, the French teacher and also the French Club adviser, had handled the travel arrangements through the Bittinger Travel Agency, which had been used for similar trips over the past two years. Three weeks before the class was scheduled to go, Jack Bittinger, the head of Bittinger Travel, suddenly disappeared for parts unknown, taking all the agency's funds, including the French Club's money. The trip didn't happen, and all the money was lost. Everybody was very upset, to say the least.

Over the next month, the school was besieged with complaints from the children's parents. Jack Bittinger was nowhere to be found, but the parents still needed someone to blame. Most of the complaints were about Mrs. Trezblidian.

"Somebody has to take responsibility for this."

"She shouldn't have been so naïve."

"She betrayed the children's trust."

A very upset Emily Trezblidian wrote a note to each family apologizing for the disaster. In her note she explained, "Mr. Bittinger sent me a travel voucher [that turned out to be completely phony] for the flight and for our accommodations. I had had no trouble with him the previous two years. I never suspected that he would do anything like this. I am deeply sorry."

But this was not enough. The complaints continued and even escalated when a few parents suggested that because of her incompetence in handling the trip, the school should consider dismissing her. The school didn't, and finally the whole incident blew over, but not before Emily Trezblidian went through a very rough few months.

"I never thought this could happen," she told a friend, sobbing.

The need to blame can be a real problem for relationships. Over the course of time, problems will inevitably arise. And regardless of whether it is the other person's fault or not, our baby self has to apportion blame.

Natalie was dropped off for her haircut at Henri D's by her daughter, Kara, so that Kara could use the car that evening. Natalie's husband, Evan, who could leave work when he wanted to on Friday afternoons, was going to pick up Natalie at five o'clock on his way home.

Natalie's haircut was finished right at five, which was when Henri D's closed for the day. Unfortunately, it was raining very hard at that point, and Natalie was not happy at all when at five thirty-five Evan pulled up in front of the salon.

"I'm sorry," said Evan. "They just started construction on I-47 and I got caught in terrible traffic."

"You should have left earlier. It's pouring. You shouldn't have taken the chance you'd be late. I'm drenched."

"I'm sorry, but I left in plenty of time. I just didn't know about the construction."

"Well, what was I supposed to do? You shouldn't have taken the chance."

"But I didn't know."

"You should have. You should have left earlier. Look at me. I'm drenched. You were inconsiderate."

"But I didn't know about the construction."

"That's not good enough."

They should have known better. They were too careless.

Bad happens, and it often happens despite everyone's good intentions and best-laid plans. Nobody can control the world; it is too big and too random. Much of the bad that happens is nobody's fault.

When bad happens, it is best to grieve and then focus on what comes next. Forget the blame; all that does is make the other person feel bad and defensive and lead to arguments that serve no useful purpose.

A story:

One day, the baby self was walking down the street when a gust of wind blew a stick in its path, causing the baby self to trip and twist its ankle slightly. The baby self immediately went to a doctor, who diagnosed it as a mild sprain.

The next day, the baby self showed up at court.

"I'm filing three separate suits. First, I'm suing the city for not having the sidewalk clear of dangerous objects that people could trip on. Second, though I have not yet found the tree, I have a suit against an as-yet-to-be-named plaintiff for not trimming potentially dangerous branches off his trees that could get blown away by the wind and cause injury. Third, I am suing Channel Six, whose weather report included nothing about possible dangerous gusts of wind that might blow objects in people's paths."

We interview the baby self.

"Do you really think that it was the fault of all those people?"

"Yes."

"You're not doing it just to get money?"

"That, too, but no, all of the people were at fault."

"You don't think that it was just unlucky chance that blew the stick in your path, causing you to trip?"

"No. Nothing is by chance. Everything bad is somebody's fault. And I don't know what your point is, but you're starting to piss me off, so maybe I'll sue you, too."

Where a serious misfortune occurs, the baby self's need to seek out someone to blame can be very destructive.

Two months after flunking out of high school because of constantly skipping class and doing no work, Gene and Trina's son, Alexander, ran off to Mexico and got into serious drug dealing.

"You were too strict with him," said Gene.

"No, you were always undermining what I was doing," said Trina.

Neither ever forgave the other for destroying their son.

Maybe Gene was right. Maybe Alexander ran away because Trina was too strict. Maybe Trina was right. Maybe he left because Gene was too lenient and undermined his wife too regularly. Maybe—probably—it had little to do with either. What was true was that both parents loved their son and were genuinely trying to do what they thought was best for him. It was a tragedy that the blaming divided them. It would have been so much nicer for both Trina and Gene if, avoiding the blame, they could have shared the sadness of having a child who turned into the opposite of everything they had hoped for.

It is a natural reaction for us to seek out someone to blame, but it is not always our best option.

Not so good:

Gary was using the garbage disposal when suddenly it stopped.

"Janis, the garbage disposal stopped again. I think there's a dishrag caught in it."

"Oh, for chrissake, Gary. Why can't you be more careful? You do this all the time."

"I wasn't using the dishrag. I didn't even see it in the sink when I turned on the garbage disposal."

"How could you not see it? You didn't even look."

"I did look. Besides, you're the one who uses the dishrags."

Better:

"Janis, the garbage disposal stopped again. I think there's a dishrag caught in it."

"Damn! Well, let me see if I can fix it."

"Thanks."

Not so good:

Clarita and Inez were planning to go to the store to buy a new dishwasher that was advertised on sale in that morning's newspaper. They were going to go out around ten that morning. However, Clarita was working on a Web page that she was designing, so they didn't leave until twelve-thirty. When they got to the store, the particular dishwasher they wanted was sold out.

"Clarita, if it wasn't for you working on your stupid project, this wouldn't have happened. You are so thoughtless. You could have done it after we got back."

"How was I to know that they were going to sell out?"

"You could have thought."

"Well, you didn't say anything. I would have gone if you had said something."

"Now you're blaming me?"

————

Better:

"Shit, now we're screwed," says Inez. "It was a really good deal."

"Yeah, I don't know if we'll see something like that again. Damn, if only I'd known, I would have postponed working on that Web page until we got back."

"Yeah, it really pisses me off. It was such a good deal."

Not so good:

(*Cough. Cough. Sneeze.*) "Now I've caught your cold. I told you to wash your hands before you touched anything that I might use."

"I'm sorry. I tried to be as careful as I could."

"Well, you weren't careful enough. I saw a number of times where you sneezed into your hands, and you just didn't want to be bothered washing them off. You are so inconsiderate."

"I did the best I could. I didn't want you to catch my cold."

"You didn't try very hard to prevent it from happening."

"What, you'd rather I went to stay at a motel?"

Better:

(*Cough. Cough. Sneeze.*) "Now I've caught your cold. I hate it when I get a cold."

"I'm sorry. I feel bad. I didn't want to give it to you. Maybe you should take a lot of vitamin C. I think it really does help limit my colds."

"Yeah, maybe I will."

I'm a Loser

Sometimes it serves the baby self's purposes to blame itself. This is a less obvious side of the baby self, its passive side, yet one that can be very destructive.

————

Lamont, just a few years out of college, was in his fourth month working for Opportunities Unlimited, a marketing research firm. He liked the job. It was interesting work, the position was a step up from his last job, and the pay was good. But the job was difficult. Opportunities Unlimited gave Lamont a lot of responsibility, not all of which he felt confident enough to handle. Some of his previous experience helped, but much was new, and he had to wing it much of the time. Lamont felt as though he were flying by the seat of his pants. He made mistakes, which his superiors noticed and were not happy with.

Then one day it was announced that the firm was updating its way of doing business. For the next two days, all employees would be trained in a new set of procedures. Lamont hadn't really mastered the old procedures. By the end of the second day of training, Lamont felt that he was sinking more than swimming. A week later, he was fired. He got two weeks' severance pay and was told to go home that day.

Lamont was devastated. It was not that he hadn't seen it coming, but he had liked the job and had tried so hard. Over the next few days, he did little—sat around his apartment, watched television, talked to a few friends.

I guess I'm just not smart enough for this kind of work. Who am I kidding? I've never done well on those standardized tests [though he had gotten pretty good grades in college]. *I always knew that I wasn't as smart as Reggie and Dalton and those guys* [high school friends]. *Dad always called me "stupid boy" whenever I screwed up. I used to hate it. But I suppose he was right.*

Over the next couple of weeks, Lamont began to rethink his plans. Rather than look for work, he thought about moving back to Maple Ridge, the suburb in another state where he grew up. Though there were marketing jobs available, Lamont did not apply for them, nor did he investigate the possibility of taking courses that might fill some of the apparent gaps in his job skills. Instead, he picked up a couple of odd jobs, and four months later he moved back to his hometown. Lamont never did go back into marketing.

In life, we fail a lot. We need to be able to deal with it and move on. The baby self takes situations that end badly and transforms them into personal character traits. *That was really hard* becomes *You are a stupid person, a loser.* Rather than *This was a really hard job, maybe it was too hard for me,* the baby self's skill at fault finding and blame switches it to *I'm a loser.* The unfortunate result is that setbacks become disasters, and stumbling blocks become proof of total incompetence.

As always, the baby self can swiftly recall corroborating evidence for its case. There are many available examples to show Lamont that he was terminally stupid and always had been. Why would the baby self do something so destructive? What could it possibly gain?

When the baby self says *I'm a loser,* it permits itself to give up, to not even try. And if you don't have to try, there is no anxiety, no worry, about what will happen. You know that nothing will happen.

To have a fulfilling life, you have to be willing regularly to put yourself on the line. Sometimes you succeed. But sometimes you will fail. Sometimes your worries will be justified.

The baby self wants none of this. Above all, the baby self abhors anxiety and will take depression over anxiety every time.

You're miserable, a total failure. You sit at home and do nothing but watch TV day after day.

So? I don't worry about stuff. That's not true. I do worry. On my TV soaps I worry whether Leslie will discover that Brad, not Cleo, was the one who kidnapped her baby; Cleo was acting suspicious on purpose to get back at Mark following her surgery. Actually, there's a lot to worry about.

The baby self, if it could, would never go out, would never take chances, and would stay in baby self mode forever. That's what it gains by being a loser.

In Lamont's case, there was a more useful, more mature approach.

Is it that I am stupid, or did Opportunities Unlimited expect too much of me too quickly? Should I give up on marketing because I'm not smart enough, or is one bad experience with Opportunities Unlimited not enough evidence? If I like marketing, shouldn't I try it somewhere else and maybe take another marketing class to improve my skills?

The baby self's overall philosophy: *Do nothing, try nothing, sounds good—as long as I get to eat and watch TV.*

The mature self's overall philosophy: *Life is hard, it has ups and downs, but far better is to keep trying than have a life of nothing.*

The baby self's defeatist stance is subtle and pervasive.

I hate being fat. I'm an ugly fat pig. Of course, if I actually lost weight, which would require a lot of effort, then I would have to worry about what other people think of how I look. This way I know. They think I look like a fat pig. So I don't have to go out in public much. Besides, this way I get to take a lot of naps.

The defeatist stance can subtly undermine relationships.

"Eliott, how can you have no money in your account? We're not going to be able to pay all our bills for this month."

"I'm sorry. I just didn't keep good track."

"But I thought you had over a thousand dollars in that account. What happened?"

"I don't know. I didn't realize how much I was spending. I'm no good at money, okay? I'm just no good at it. I'm dumb."

"You're not dumb."

"Yeah, I am. I'm stupid. I can't do money. I just can't."

Eliott's defeatist stance short-circuits any useful discussion about money and any potential changes that could be made. The problem will continue.

Melinda had accepted an invitation for herself and Shannon to go out with Karyn and Anyssa that Saturday night. When she told Shannon about it, Shannon was mad.

"You knew I wanted to go to the shore this weekend. That was really inconsiderate of you. You make decisions that affect both of us and you don't even consult me. There are two of us, you know?"

"I'm a bad person, okay? I'm a selfish, bad person."

"But you always do this. You can't just decide whatever you want. You have to think of me."

"I'm a bad person, all right?"

Melinda's sweeping statement about how she's a bad person avoids any genuine discussion about her selfish decision making.

Both are stories of cop-outs. Rather than entering into a real discussion, the baby self stance accomplishes two nice baby self aims: *I don't have to get into an uncomfortable discussion, and I don't have to actually try to change my behavior.*

The bad consequence is that problem issues are not dealt with. Nothing changes, nothing moves into a potentially new and better direction. One person's refusal to tackle problems can become increasingly frustrating for his or her partner. Relationships can stagnate.

What to do?

Recognize that your baby self avoids difficult situations that might prove stressful. For your baby self, the easiest way is always the best way.

To combat your baby self, ask yourself this question:

Is it that I am really a loser, or is it that I just don't want to try?

Again, we cannot eliminate the voice of our baby self, but it is useful to recognize it for what it is.

Baby self: *It's not a bad thing that happened. It's that I'm a total loser.*

Mature self: *Yes, it is a bad thing that happened. But I'll try to deal with it and do what I can so that the same bad thing won't happen in the future.*

Accept Blame? Never!

The baby self will accept blame, but only to get out of having to do anything.

Yes, it was my fault that I didn't rake the leaves. I couldn't do it because my back is acting up so much. I guess it's chronic, and I will never be able to rake leaves or, for that matter, do anything hard ever again.

But otherwise, the baby self in us never accepts blame. Blame makes us feel bad. Further, it means taking responsibility for our own behavior, and that might have unpleasant consequences.

"You spilled the milk?"

"No. I didn't."

"You have to clean it up."

"But I didn't spill it."

"The glass is in your hand and I just saw you spill it."

"No, you didn't."

As adults, when we are accused of wrongdoing, our blame-deflecting mechanisms come immediately to the fore. As you know, accepting blame and letting it simply sit there is very hard indeed.

"Yes, it was my fault, but . . ."

And then we explain why it wasn't actually our fault. Or we explain how what we did wasn't actually bad. Or we say anything.

Yet there is a great advantage in life to the unqualified owning up to mistakes.

"I'm sorry, you're right, that was a stupid thing for me to have said."

Or perhaps simply, "I'm sorry, I'll try not to do it again."

The advantage of fully owning up to mistakes without qualifications is that others respond to you better and you get to act with more integrity. It is amazing the degree to which in real life the unqualified owning up of one's mistakes works so much better, has such a better outcome, goes over so much better with others. It is also amazing, especially given all this, how difficult it is for anybody to do it.

"What's that?"

"It's a deluxe, fully equipped mobile home, and it's all yours, absolutely free, if you can say any of the following and add on nothing whatsoever. No qualifiers. No embellishments."

"Sounds easy."

"Are you ready?"

"Yeah."

"Here's the list."

I'm sorry. It was a mistake. I shouldn't have done it.

I'm sorry. I was stupid.

I'm sorry. I was thoughtless.

"Okay, now you try it."

"No problem. This is so easy. Mobile home, here I come. Open your door, baby, 'cause Daddy's comin' home. Here I go.

"I'm sorry. It was a mistake. I shouldn't have done it. It was a mistake. I make mistakes sometimes. I'm not perfect. Nobody's perfect. Everybody makes some mistakes. That's part of being human. Actually, I shouldn't be blamed at all, because this was one of my allotted human mistakes. In fact, my admitting it makes me a good person, and I should be admired, not blamed. . . . Do I get the mobile home?"

"Not quite."

Not so good:

"You said you'd take out the trash."

"I'm sorry. I've had a lot of other stuff to do."

Better:

"You said you'd take out the trash."

"I'm sorry. I'll do it right now."

Not so good:

"Harrison, I almost tripped over your briefcase."

"I'm sorry, I just put it down for a second when I got in. I was about to move it."

Better:

"Harrison, I almost tripped over your briefcase."

"I'm sorry. I'll move it right now."

Not so good:

"You shouldn't have yelled at me."

"I'm sorry, but sometimes you really piss me off. I can't help it."

Better:

"You shouldn't have yelled at me."

"I'm sorry."

It is not easy. But with practice you do get better at it, and the outcomes are so much better.

Let me give a tougher example, one that happens frequently within relationships. It is when we may have done something truly wrong, but the other person did something wrong, too—maybe not then, but something comparable on another occasion.

Doesn't this then excuse me from blame? I mean, if she did the same as I did or something like it, isn't it then only fair, or at least not my fault, what I did this time?

That is, we resort to the fairness balancing scale. Confronted with blame, we make use of that scale and absolve ourselves from fault.

Yes, I did do it, but you can't really blame me, because after all, she . . .

At a party, Iris told a story about a time that she and her husband, Clayton, were at the mall and he was supposed to meet her at a specific time and place, and he kept screwing up. In the course of the story, Iris referred to Clayton as "Mr. Stupid." From then on, it became a joke that Iris would sometimes make about Clayton doing bonehead things. At those times, she would refer to him as "Mr. Stupid." The Mr. Stupid character was not part of their relationship outside these gatherings of good friends. Clayton never particularly liked it, but he did not hate it, either. He felt a little embarrassed whenever Iris referred to him as Mr. Stupid, but he never cared enough to make an issue out of it, knowing that Iris did not intend to be mean-spirited.

Then one Saturday evening at the Brentmeyers', Clayton was telling a story to Weedy and Aaron Lavasseur. Iris was sitting next to him.

"Well, you know how testy our daughter, Charlotte, can be. Anyway, it was supposed to be her birthday dinner and she loves Iris's lasagna, but dumb-dumb here forgot to turn on the oven. And, omigod, did we hear it from Princess Charlotte.

" 'My birthday is ruined,' " said Clayton, mimicking Charlotte's voice. The Lavasseurs laughed.

As soon as they were in the car on the way home, Iris lit into Clayton. "What the hell did you think you were doing?"

"What?"

"You called me a dumb-dumb. Right in front of the Lavasseurs. I suppose you thought you were being cute, but I was humiliated. I can't believe you said that."

"I was only joking."

"You were showing off. I felt so embarrassed in front of Weedy and Aaron."

"I was only joking. I didn't mean anything by it."

"You don't get it. Even joking, it's degrading. It's a put-down. You don't say that kind of thing about a woman, especially your wife—ever."

"Wait a minute. What about all the times you've called me Mr. Stupid? It's all right for you, but it's not all right for me?"

Here, of course, is the baby self's ledger. These countering examples automatically pop into our head the moment we are accused of anything.

She calls me Mr. Stupid, so that gives me the right to call her a dumb-dumb. It's only fair.

This is where Clayton gets into trouble. He is right: There is an imbalance. It is unfair. But that's not the point. The point is that Iris does not like Clayton putting her down, even if it is only in jest. Iris was offended by what Clayton said, and she told him so. Clayton should not try to justify what he did. Rather, he should accept the fact that his words offended his wife.

The better response from Clayton would have been: "I'm sorry. I'll try to be more careful in the future." End of comment.

Nothing is gained when we refer to the baby self's ledger. Our accuser only gets angrier, and we come off as a baby who can't take responsibility for our actions.

Later, if Clayton wants to bring up the issue of Iris's calling him Mr. Stupid, he can. But he should do so only if he genuinely wants Iris not to call him Mr. Stupid anymore and not as payback for her anger at him.

And, should he bring it up, Clayton must not connect it to the dumb-dumb issue.

When you did something wrong, you did something wrong. Period.

Wrongly Accused

What if you are accused of a wrongdoing when you genuinely did nothing wrong? What if your accuser does not believe you are innocent and nothing you say seems able to change his or her view?

Monica and Luke were planning to go shopping. Monica was watching a movie on television. As soon as the movie ended, they left. Monica always attended to cat issues, but in her hurry to leave she had failed to check whether the door to the bathroom—where they kept the litter box—was open.

On returning from shopping later that day: "Luke, there's cat shit all over the rug. You didn't check to make sure the bathroom door was open."

"What are you talking about? You always check it. I didn't even think to do it."

"You knew we were going to leave as soon as the movie I was watching was over. I can't always take responsibility for everything."

"That's not fair. I *do* take responsibility. It's just that you always take care of everything about Rascal. I didn't think about it because you always do it."

"That's my point. I have to take responsibility for everything. And now there's cat shit on the rug."

"That's not fair, Monica. You've always taken care of the cat. I take responsibility for lots of other stuff."

"If you *really* took responsibility, you'd know that I can't always do everything. It's your fault Rascal made the mess."

His protests going nowhere, Luke stormed out of the room.

"You better clean up that cat shit," Monica called out after him.

Luke, who did not feel like getting into a further argument, did clean up the mess. But he fumed to himself for the rest of the day.

How dare Monica blame me for what was her fault? She always takes care of the cat. This has nothing to do with responsibility. How dare she blame me? It was her fault.

The next day, Luke told the story to his friend Mike. Mike agreed that it was Monica's fault. That night, still stewing, Luke brought it up again.

"I told Mike the story about the cat shit, and he agreed with me that no way was it my fault."

"Luke, you are a crazy person. What business is it of Mike's? Besides, he agrees with anything you say."

"Well, it wasn't my fault."

"It *was* your fault. When are you going to grow up?"

Luke stewed all the more.

It wasn't my fault. It was hers, and she absolutely doesn't see it.

Our whole being screams for at least some recognition of the injustice.

If only I could get on The Oprah Winfrey Show, thought Luke.

"Hi, everybody. Good to have you here. Today we have Luke and Monica, a couple from Portsmouth, New Hampshire. You had a problem about your cat, Rascal, is that right?"

Luke told his side of the story, then Monica told hers.

"Well, this *is* unusual," said Oprah. "For the first time ever, our audience poll was unanimous. Our entire studio audience feels that Luke, you were right. And frankly, I think so, too."

"Yes!" said Luke.

"Oh, my goodness! Our instant Internet poll of viewers is unanimous for you, too."

"I guess I was wrong," Monica said in a small voice. "I'm sorry, Luke."

Cheers from the studio audience.

Unfortunately, it is very difficult to get on *The Oprah Winfrey Show.* And in truth, had Luke and Monica gone on such a show, it would have created more, not less, of a rift between them. Will Luke ever be able to get Monica to see the light? Not in real life.

But our baby self screams for at least some recognition of our plight. As discussed, we desperately want to bring it before a judge, any judge.

To Marilyn, a friend at a party: "I want you to listen to a story. Monica, let's see what Marilyn thinks."

To Herbert, Luke's father-in-law: "What do you think? Monica, let me tell your father the story and see what he thinks."

To the telephone number information person: "I do want a phone number. But you seem like a nice and intelligent person, and before I ask you for the number—I know this may seem a little unusual—I really would like your opinion about something."

What to do?

You can tell a friend. But only if you do not bring the friend's reaction back to the original arena. That just creates more trouble. Your friend is only someone you are using to validate your feelings, not a judge.

If it truly bothers you, the best thing to do is to let your accuser know what you think, state your case, present your arguments, and then disengage.

"I'm not the one who is wrong. You're wrong. And this is why. . . . But you just don't see it."

Then close your argument.

The great baby self error is not in presenting the case, but in trying too hard to win it. What remains on the table are two conflicting opinions, which is not so bad. As long as you know that the other person knows that you absolutely disagree.

I can't convince her that she was wrong, but she can't convince me that I was wrong, either.

In every relationship, there will always be discord that resurfaces periodically. The fabric of any relationship has holes in it; there is no such thing as perfection. I will have more to say about this in the next section.

Part III

Accepting Less

Chapter 8

When They Aren't Exactly Whom You Wanted

Changing What You Got

Nobody's perfect. You can't expect them to be. That's easy to say, but not always so easy to accept.

Often, we interpret the bad behavior of others as evidence of a character flaw or, even worse, an indicator that they are someone less than what we had wanted: a disappointment.

Grace and Arthur left the supermarket and were loading their groceries into the car. Arthur liked to put the bags of groceries in any which way and be on the road as quickly as possible. Grace, on the other hand, liked to put the groceries in more carefully, lest the bags fall over and the groceries spill out during the ride home. After putting the bags in the car, Arthur climbed into the driver's seat. However, Grace lingered to rearrange them in the back. Arthur squirmed impatiently. Finally, satisfied that the bags were reasonably secure, Grace went to get in the passenger seat. But as she opened the door, she paused and looked down at the side of the car.

"Did you notice this, Arthur? It looks like there's a little paint chipped off on the side down here." Grace bent down to get a closer look.

"Will you get in the car!" said Arthur in a loud, impatient, and bossy tone of voice.

"What?" said Grace, standing up quickly.

Arthur, knowing he had stepped over the line, attempted damage control. "Would you please get in the car. I'll look at it when we get home. I promise."

But Grace was not appeased. She got in the car and said nothing during the fifteen-minute drive back to the house.

Arriving home: "Who do you think you are that you can talk to me that way?"

"I'm sorry, I shouldn't have yelled," Arthur said as he got out of the car. "Let me look and see if the paint's chipped."

"You're just never going to learn, are you."

"I said I was sorry."

"You just don't understand, do you. You can't talk to somebody that way, ever."

"I said I was sorry. What more do you want from me?"

"That's not the way you talk to somebody you care about. You know it's wrong, but you do it anyway."

"I said I was sorry I raised my voice. I shouldn't have. I'll try not to do it again."

"You don't get it. You can't be like that with me."

"I'm sorry. I said I was sorry."

"You really don't care, do you? You just say whatever you hope is going to shut me up."

"I don't know what you want me to say."

"I don't want you to *say* anything. That's the point. I want you to get it."

"I know what you want. You should have married your father."

The discussion deteriorated from there.

Grace wants something that she is not going to get. She wants to change Arthur. She wants to change not just what he does, but who he is. She wants a partner who *really* understands, who is so in touch with how she feels that he would never do anything completely insensitive, never act toward her in the self-centered, impatient manner Arthur just had.

He's just too self-centered, too insensitive. He needs to understand how his actions make me feel. If he did, he would never have acted that way. I have to get him to change.

People don't change. They're the unreturnable item you picked out at the store and brought home. They may gradually learn to act differently, perhaps even mature a little, maybe even see things differently. But they are who they are. This is a reality that the baby self in us never accepts. We all want a perfect partner, someone we can always trust, who always puts us first and is always there for us. Grace's baby self pushes to get the perfect Arthur, but in doing so, she short-circuits another, far more healthy process.

He's such a jerk. I hate it when he acts like this. I really hate it. And he's never going to change. I have a husband who can really act like a jerk. This is what I am stuck with.

Obviously, this is a depressing thought.

What I have is less than what I had wanted.

But there is an importance in recognizing this depressing fact —and it is depressing, no question about it. Only after having that thought, that realization—grieving for and accepting that it is a loss—can we move on to a next stage.

I hate it when he acts like a jerk. I will always hate it, but overall *I guess he's okay. I could do worse.*

From this, it becomes possible to love this flawed person. It becomes possible to get past those times when he truly does act like a jerk. If the bad times are too frequent, too much of who he is, that is a different story, and much tougher decisions may have to be made. But the depressing realization *He has all these flaws. He is not completely what I wanted* is the absolute and necessary step that allows us to move past getting stuck forever trying to change whom we got.

With any long-term love relationship, we do not see the person we love as perfect. We see them as flawed. Yet we love them anyway.

How can that be?

John and Lydia have been together for fifteen years.

"John, I have a deal for you. I know how you hate it when Lydia nags you. If you want, I'm going to give you—starting right now—a Lydia who never nags you. Not ever."

"Sounds great, but let me think about it."

"No, you have to decide now or the deal is off."

"She never nags?"

"That's the deal."

"I don't know."

"What do you mean, you don't know? I thought you hated the nagging?"

"I do. But if she never nagged, it wouldn't be Lydia. It would be weird. Like she had a lobotomy or something."

"You mean you wouldn't like it if she never nagged?"

"No. Like I said, if she never nagged, it wouldn't be Lydia. It would be like trying to love somebody totally different."

"I heard that," said Lydia, who was listening outside the door. "You like that I nag."

"You weren't supposed to hear it. You said she wouldn't hear it."

"Oops. I guess we screwed up. Sorry."

In any long-term love relationship, the one we love has flaws and we love them anyway.

But with the baby self running the show, flaws are not an option, so with each instance of bad behavior, it pushes for change—now. *I need to know. I need to see proof that we will change.*

The baby self says: "Why can't you understand? You have to understand. I want to see that you understand."

"I said I understand."

"No, you're just saying that to appease me."

But if you can get to that next step, grieve over what you wished you got but didn't, then a much easier scenario opens up. This one has a much more realistic goal.

"You are such a jerk. You really are."

But that's it.

I don't want anything from you. I just want you to know that you acted like a real jerk. And I hope you won't act this way again.

Having been told, maybe Arthur will act that way less. Maybe he won't. He is still Arthur.

So what do you do when they misbehave? Get mad. Let them know how mad you are. And then move on. But you can move on only when you have already grieved. For only then, even as you strongly express your displeasure, will this other thought click in: *There he goes again, acting like a jerk.* And with the thought comes the accompanying feeling—resignation, but not depression: *This is what I got. But I'm going to keep her.*

Get mad. Let them know how you feel. But then move on.

Other Couples Always Seem to Have It Better

In the last chapter, we saw that we can be happy with what we have, even if it is not quite as good as what we might have wanted. We *can* be satisfied with less than perfect. But one thing can suddenly make us feel not as good about what we have: seeing somebody who seems to have it better.

Stephie and Reggie were not a perfect couple, but they lived with it. They accepted, more or less, the fact that their relationship left something to be desired. But whenever they spent time with their friends Fred and Sylvia, the failings in their own relationship became bitterly apparent.

One evening, Stephie and Reggie were talking.

"Fred and Sylvia's relationship can't be as perfect as it seems, can it? Wouldn't it be good to know that they have their problems, too, just like us?"

"Yeah, if I could only know that, I know it would make me feel a whole lot better about us."

"Me too. Do you think we should talk to them?"

"Yeah."

They did.

"We have some questions we want to ask you."

"Sure."

"Reggie and I can't help noticing that the two of you seem really supportive of each other. Is it like that all the time with you guys?"

"Yeah. Wouldn't you say so, pumpkins?"

"Yeah, definitely."

"Well, what about being considerate? We always notice each of you thinking about the other before you do anything. You don't always do that, right?"

"No, I think I always pretty much do. You do that, too, right, Fred?"

"Yeah, pretty much always. Yeah."

"Hunh. Well, it always looks like each of you really seems to get pleasure from what the other says. Each of you seems to enjoy listening, even more than when you're talking yourself. It can't be that way always, right?"

"I don't know. I think I always like hearing what Sylvia has to say. How about you, dear?"

"Yeah. Frankly, I'd rather listen to Fred than talk myself."

"Oh."

Who are these couples, anyway? Do they really exist? Or is it true that they have been placed on earth by the devil to make ordinary folk like you and me feel bad?

We see others who seem to have it better than us. It is part of human nature to compare and feel dissatisfied. The good news is that these feelings of jealousy do fade with time and distance.

Yeah, I guess maybe Fred and Sylvia do have it better, but we have it okay. Sometimes pretty good.

On the other hand, as everybody knows:

Who am I to complain? Think about all the starving children in Africa.

Doesn't really help at all—ever.

"Well, at least their nice mahogany dining room table isn't as perfect as it used to be," Reggie commented later that evening.

"Yeah, it's really too bad your accidentally spilling that liquid bleach on it."

"Yeah."

I Shouldn't Have to Ask (If He Really Cared About Me)

"And from this day forward forever shall we both be as one, I for you and so, thou, my beloved, for me. Thy wants are the wants of my heart, my hopes are as a part of thy own desires. Two hearts as one."

It was eleven p.m. Mary Alice and I had been driving for four hours. We had just gotten off I-95 and now faced another two hours of driving up the Maine coast to my father's house in Rockport. Ahead on our right flashed the sign MOONLIGHTER MOTEL—VACANCY.

It is a well-known fact in my family that because I am cheap, I do not want to spend the money for a motel if I don't have to. It is also well-known that I like driving late at night and do not mind at all driving the extra two hours. It is also a well-known fact that Mary Alice is not cheap, and after four hours of driving, at eleven p.m. she much prefers to stop and drive the remainder in the morning. Without a word, I drove past the motel.

There will probably be some more motels. We can stop in a little while if Mary Alice really wants to. Besides, she didn't say anything when we saw the motel, so she probably doesn't want to stop that much.

It was the last motel between there and Rockport.

About half an hour later, no motels in sight, Mary Alice said, "You should have stopped."

"I would have if you had said anything."

"You knew I wanted to stop."

"But you didn't say anything."

"You knew."

Mary Alice was right, of course. She shouldn't have had to ask. I knew, but I didn't want to stop, and because she didn't actually *tell* me to stop, didn't that mean I was allowed to keep driving?

As the result of numerous similar occurrences, Mary Alice came to the conclusion early in our marriage that I was far from perfect, but she chose to stay married to me anyway. As a result, she asks:

"Sweetheart, would you please roll up the window?"

I had rolled it down inch by inch, hoping she wouldn't notice.

"Since you're going to the store, check and see if we need milk, and if we do, get some."

I had tried to sneak out without Mary Alice noticing. After all, to check about the milk, I'd have to bend down a little to look into the rear of the refrigerator, and my back has been bothering me. Really, it has.

That they have to ask can get to be a serious sticking point between couples. Many feel that there is something lost when they have to ask. They are not incorrect. There is a closeness, a special shared intimacy, when this other person who knows you and cares about you can anticipate your wants without your having to say anything. The problem is that in any long-term relationship, this does not always happen.

Kendra and Tarik were very much in love. They were planning to move in together, and both envisioned the day they would marry and be together forever. They liked to go to the movies. Tarik liked to sit way up front. Kendra liked to sit in the back. The first time they went to the movies together, as soon as they got into the theater Tarik said that he wanted to sit up front. Kendra said nothing, and they sat up front; Kendra didn't mind it that much, but she didn't like it that much, either. It became their pattern—sitting up front. Still, Kendra didn't say anything because she was falling in love with Tarik and wanted him to be happy.

But as time went on and the relationship developed, Kendra began to think that at least some of the time she would like to sit in the back. But even then she didn't say anything. She didn't want to say anything because she didn't want to *have* to say anything. She wanted Tarik to one day ask if she was okay with sitting in the front. She hinted:

"Doesn't it hurt your neck sitting up front like this?"

"I think I got a little headache tonight from sitting so close in the theater."

"Unh, my back's a little stiff from sitting up here. I'm going to walk around for a bit. I'll be back."

"Boy, up this close, everybody looks sort of ugly."

But Tarik never said anything.

I know it's a little thing, but if he really cared about me, wasn't quite so focused on himself, wouldn't he have asked at least one time?

Kendra began to notice other things. Tarik didn't ask her if she wanted anything when he went into the kitchen to get himself a snack. He ordered before her in restaurants. Little things. And Kendra wouldn't say anything, but she would notice, hoping Tarik would be more considerate of her. And when Kendra finally did start to speak up, she complained and they argued.

They never did move in together.

Kendra's relationship was ruined by the less obvious side of the baby self, its passive side. This side wants the world—Mommy and Daddy—to look out for you, always magically to know and provide for all your wants. To have to ask spoils all of that. But sometimes you do have to ask, or else you just don't receive.

Mary Alice learned.

"When we get to the next town, I want you to stop at the first motel we see."

"But we're only two and a half hours from Denver, and I know that they'll have a bigger selection of motels there that I'm sure you'll like better."

"I want you to stop in the next town. And don't sulk."

Why would Mary Alice think I would sulk? I'm way above anything like that.

Chapter 9

Friends, Relatives

Our baby self, who accepts only perfection, has unrealistic expectations not only of our nearest and dearest, but of friends and adult siblings as well.

Friends, however, often will let you down, will disappoint you, will not come through, or will make you feel insulted. What the baby self in us cannot accept is that friends have their own lives and their own priorities, and they do not always put us first. Not only that, they have flaws . . . and sometimes those flaws cause them to act like inconsiderate jerks—even to us, their dear friend.

When They Let You Down

Being let down is the one "crime" within the realm of friendship that our baby self has the most trouble with. Many friendships survive nonethe-

"flounder"

less, but some don't. Many <u>founder</u> where maybe they didn't have to, because our baby self just couldn't get past the disappointment.

Armand had told a customer that he would deliver some shingles to him on Tuesday by noon. But when he went out to his truck that Tuesday morning, the starter had died. There was no way Armand could get the truck fixed and deliver the shingles that same day as he had promised. Armand called his brother, Clement.

"I'm really fucked unless I can get the shingles over to this guy by noon. Could you bring your truck over and we can load up the shingles? I swear we'll be done by eleven-thirty at the latest."

"Shit," said Clement. "I don't know. I got a lot of stuff I have to do today. Let me get back to you in ten minutes."

Clement owned his own business, and it was possible for him to go over to Armand's that morning, but he had a busy day scheduled and would be very inconvenienced. Armand often had crises like these. He and his wife, Jeannette, lived more or less hand to mouth. Armand was never really organized enough to start getting ahead. Clement did not mind occasionally bailing out his brother; he liked his brother and did want to help him when he could. But on this particular day, he really didn't want to. Armand was just going to have to fend for himself.

Clement called Armand back. "No, Armand, I just can't do it today. I'm sorry. I have too much stuff that I need to do. I'm sorry, I can't."

"But Jesus Christ, Clement, what the fuck am I supposed to do? I promised this guy."

"I don't know what to tell you, I just can't do it today."

"Well, thanks a lot. Thanks a fucking lot," said Armand, slamming down the phone.

I can't count on him. He's my brother, and I can't count on him. I know I ask for stuff, but when I really needed him, he didn't come through. He knows I need every piece of work I can get. He and Anne have it good. I don't even know if I can make the fucking payments on the truck.

But Clement was mad, too.

Why can't he get his life together? What is his problem? I'm always bailing him out. I don't even know if he appreciates it. He just expects that I'm always going to be there ready to drop everything because he screwed up again. He takes advantage of me, and I let him.

Nonetheless, Wednesday night Clement called Armand to see how he made out.

"Yeah, well, like I said, thanks a lot. I couldn't get the shingles to the guy until today, and he was really pissed. And now he's making a big fucking fuss about whether he's going to pay me."

"It's not my job always to have to bail you out of every piece of shit you get in," Clement said angrily.

"Well, I guess not, I guess fucking not." And again Armand slammed down the phone.

That's what I got, a brother who helps when it's convenient for him, to make himself feel good so he can say to himself that he helps out his pathetic asshole of a brother that he's so much better than. But if I really need him, and it doesn't fit his schedule, he shows his true colors. Well, no, thank you. I don't need his fucking charity. I thought that I could count on him, that he was my brother. But I guess not.

Clement fumed after the phone call as well:

When is he going to grow up? He thinks that when he screws up, I should always drop everything and bail him out. He's like a fucking eight-year-old. I think I've made a mistake helping him all the time. He can't keep going through life like he's some kind of little kid. I'm not going to be part of it.

Matters cooled between the brothers, and they had only limited contact over the next few months. But they were both too fond of each other to let the animosity continue. Gradually they did start talking, and within six months they were back to exactly the same relationship they had previously.

In this story, neither brother really did anything wrong. Armand did regularly call on his brother for help, but that was because most of the time his brother gave it. Clement obviously had a right to say no, but when he did, Armand was very unhappy about it. As inevitably happens in life, there are instances in which people disappoint you. The problem is that in such situations the baby self always wants to make more of it.

As discussed, one of the most self-defeating baby self characteristics is taking an instance of disappointment and turning it into something bigger: not an isolated instance of negative behavior, but a pattern with deep meaning. Not a bad thing that happened, but a totally unacceptable thing that happened. And what so often gets lost is the actual reality, which more often than not is that there has been one negative instance in what is basically a positive relationship.

No, this is not a negative instance in what is otherwise a positive relationship. This is a deal breaker. How can I possibly keep a friendship going with someone who would treat me that way? What can they possibly think of me if they would ever do that?

Think about it. Armand's baby self, understandably frustrated by his brother's refusal to help, interpreted the incident as a betrayal.

If he really cared, if he was a true brother, he would always be there if I need him.

Yet there is another, truer, way of looking at it that gets drowned out by the baby self's fussing.

I can't count on him completely. I wish I could. Still, most of the time is a lot better than none of the time. I'm pissed off at him right now. But it's still a pretty good deal.

Clement's baby self changed the issue of an occasionally ungrateful brother into *He thinks I owe him, when I'm the one who's doing him the favor. I'm not going to let him take advantage of me anymore. Besides, it just enables him. Fuck him.*

But again there was a larger, more mature perspective.

Sometimes I'm going to say no. And when I do, Armand always acts like a jerk, which pisses me off. But I still like being able to help him when I can.

But the baby self can never see it as a negative instance in an otherwise good relationship. Why would the baby self make a big deal out of every disappointment? The answer of course is that it wants everything. Some or less than perfect are not baby self options. Hence the infamous and amazingly self-defeating stance of the baby self:

If I can't have it totally the way I want it, then I don't want it at all.

In a six-year-old we easily recognize this as childish sulking. Unfortunately, as adults we often see the same statement as an important truth that needs to be stood by.

It's not that I'm being a baby about it. I really think it's a mistake for me to deal with somebody who is going to treat me that way.

What is a friendship? Is it something based in a deep, sacred bond? Maybe. But can a friendship also be about enjoying talking to someone and spending time in their company? Do we maybe expect too much, so that when we are disappointed, we overreact?

A real friend would never . . .

Maybe, but what about somebody you have fun being with but who has flaws and for whom you are not an absolute top priority?

I would never neglect to call Charlene on her birthday, but this year she didn't call me. She gave some kind of lame excuse, but I could tell the truth was she couldn't be bothered.

Yeah, well, actually Angie is right. I thought about calling her, but I was a little tired and I just didn't do it. I knew she would be disappointed, but frankly, I didn't have the energy. I mean, it's not like she's my mother or something.

Unacceptable! At least to our baby self.

What to do?

When others disappoint you, there is one question you should always ask yourself:

Is it really so bad, is it so unforgivably terrible, or is it just less than what I wanted?

Following are some examples of when to break off a friendship and when not to.

Some reasons to break off a friendship:

1. They constantly put you down.
2. They intentionally told a false story about you to make themselves look good, and it damaged another relationship that you care about.
3. When you are with them, you usually don't enjoy yourself.
4. They stole money from you.
5. They frequently get very mad and say hurtful things to you.

Some reasons not to break off a friendship:

1. They regularly cheat on a shared luncheon bill.
2. They didn't visit you when you were in the hospital.
3. They canceled vacation plans that they had made with you, screwing up your plans.
4. Something that you told to them in confidence they told to another friend.
5. At her daughter's bat mitzvah, she put you at a table made up solely of elderly relatives instead of at the table with most of your mutual friends.

The examples in the second list may cause you to like them less. Your relationship with them may be diminished in your eyes. You may become more selective about what you do and say with them. But was what they did so bad that you should end the whole relationship?

Again, ask yourself, *Is it really so bad that I can't be friends with them anymore, or is this really about me wanting more than I am going to get?*

If you want, let them know how you felt about it. But this instance of hurt may not be worth ending the friendship.

We Take Everything Personally

We all have trouble when friends disappoint us. But one common mistake we all make is to take it personally. Their bad behavior becomes a description of us rather than a description of them. What they have done says something about us rather than about them.

Disrespect

One Friday evening, Vinnie was drinking with a couple of buddies at the Green Lantern. Vinnie had had a few beers but was far from drunk. Looking around, Vinnie inadvertently exchanged glances with a guy he had never seen before who was sitting farther down the bar.

"You got a problem?" said the guy, who clearly had had a lot to drink.

"No."

"You got some kind of fucking problem? Hey, faggot, I'm talking to you."

Vinnie got up and walked over to the guy. "Were you talking to me?"

"Yeah," said the guy, turning to face Vinnie. "Are you a faggot? You look like a faggot."

Vinnie took a swing at the guy, who partially deflected Vinnie's punch and grabbed Vinnie. The two men got into a full-fledged fight. The police were called, and both men were charged with disorderly conduct. The guy had to get stitches on the back of his head where it had hit the edge of the bar during the fight, and Vinnie had a split lip. In the end, neither got into serious trouble, but Vinnie had to go to court, and the whole thing ended up costing him $1,500.

Vinnie had two ways to interpret what the guy who had had a lot to drink said to him—one useful, one not so useful:

"You got some kind of a fucking problem? Hey, faggot, I'm talking to you."

One interpretation is:

There is a drunk guy saying unpleasant things to me.

The logical course of action dictated by this interpretation is:

I should have as little to do with him as possible, especially consider-ing he is a drunken asshole.

The other interpretation would be:

That guy thinks I'm a wimp, and if I don't respond somehow, it will show that I am a wimp.

The course of action dictated by this interpretation:

I have to show the guy I'm not a wimp.

Vinnie chose interpretation number two.

This example is pretty straightforward.

Is what happened about me, or is it about him?

Another example:

Julia was visiting Andrea at her apartment when the phone rang.

"Excuse me," said Andrea after answering the phone. "It's my friend Reenie. I haven't talked to her in a while. I won't talk long."

But in fact Andrea talked for an hour while Julia sat around twiddling her thumbs and looking at old magazines. As the minutes ticked by, Julia grew more and more irritated.

What does she think I am? Some kind of wind-up doll that just sits here until she decides to play with me?

Julia should have left or, even better, as the phone conversation dragged on, she could have said, "Listen, do you want me to leave, or are you going to finish the call soon?"

Julia did neither. Many of us probably would have done the same, thinking that Andrea would hang up in a minute. *I'll give her another five minutes. I'm sure she'll hang up by then.*

When Andrea finally hung up a full sixty-seven minutes later, Julia snapped at her.

"What were you doing, Andrea? I've been sitting here for an hour. What can you possibly have been thinking? That was really rude."

"I'm sorry, Julia," said Andrea, not sounding sorry at all. "I said it was my friend Reenie. I hadn't talked to her in six months."

"But I was here. You don't do that when you have a guest."

"Well, excuse me! You should have said something. I thought that you were okay with me talking to Reenie. I mean, I haven't spoken to her in six months."

Andrea didn't get it at all.

They argued a little more, and then Julia, totally frustrated with her friend, went home. There, she fumed.

I can't believe Andrea. She totally disrespected me. Who does she think I am that she can talk to her friend for an hour and just leave me sitting there?

The next time they talked, Julia was still angry.

"You made me just sit there for an hour. You can't treat somebody that way."

But Andrea just got hostile.

"Get over it, Julia. Really."

Again, later, Julia fussed to herself.

She acts like I'm the one with the problem. She doesn't have a clue. I can't be friends with somebody who has no respect for me at all.

Julia didn't get over it. She felt her friend's lack of respect for her was something that she could not get past. Their relationship continued, but on a much more limited basis. It was never the same.

Let's go back in time. Julia is now home, having just left Andrea's, and she is fussing about her friend's lack of respect.

We appear.

"Julia, guess what?"

"What?"

"Andrea is really self-centered."

"Tell me about it."

"That's it. Andrea's really self-centered. Always has been. Always will be."

"Yeah?"

"So what should you do if you want to be friends with a totally self-centered person?"

"Not be friends with her?"

"Possibly."

"Punch her in the face whenever she acts like a jerk?"

"You could."

"Just take shit from her all the time?"

"No, because then the relationship wouldn't be any fun."

"So what's the answer?"

"When she acts too self-centered, stand up for yourself. But also realize that her acting self-centered doesn't say anything about you. It's about her. She's self-centered. When Andrea acts that way, make sure that you let her know you don't like her behavior."

"I did that."

"Good. It might make her mad at the time."

"Yeah, it did."

"But it will set some limits—at least when she is with you. Remember, the flaw is in her, not in you."

"You're a very wise person," said Julia.

We left, admiring Julia's perceptiveness.

The baby self takes everything personally. Being the center of its universe, it knows no other way. The concept of disrespect is one of its more successful ways of transforming unpleasantness from someone else into a statement about itself:

Thus, *He sure was unpleasant* or *She sure can be a jerk sometimes* gets transformed into: *He acts like I'm a loser* and *She thinks she can get away with treating me this way.*

What to do? Always ask these questions:

Is it about me, or is it about him?

Is it about him acting bad, or is it about something wrong with me?

Being Used—I'm Always the One Who Has to Call

Here's an example similar to the last one, but which uses a variation of disrespect that all too regularly disturbs or even ends relationships. It is the idea of being taken advantage of, of being used.

Lisa called her friend Kelly.

"Hi, Kelly. It's Lisa. I was wondering. I have a half day tomorrow. Are you free? We could meet for lunch at the Lamplighter."

"I'd love that. Sure."

"Is twelve-thirty okay?"

"Yeah, that's great. I'll see you then."

The next day, Kelly and Lisa had lunch together, sat around talking, and left the restaurant around three o'clock. Both women had a good time. But afterward, Lisa couldn't stop thinking about something that had occurred to her before:

Why is it always me who has to call her? I cannot think of a time when she called me to do anything.

The more Lisa thought about it, the more annoyed she became.

I like it when we're together, but I really think she uses me. I am the one who keeps the relationship going. If I didn't call her, I don't know if there would be a relationship. If she really cared about me, wasn't so much into herself, she would take the initiative—at least some of the time. I really think she takes advantage of me. She doesn't work. She just lets things come to her as if she expects everybody else to take care of her needs. She's certainly that way with her husband. Well, I don't know if I feel like being another of her serving people. I think I'll wait and see if she ever calls me.

Lisa did wait. Months went by. And, just as Lisa had expected, Kelly didn't call. When she thought about it, Lisa only got angrier.

I don't need to have friends like that.

They didn't run into each other regularly, and now, without the scheduled meetings, Kelly gradually drifted out of Lisa's life.

A couple of years later, Lisa saw Kelly again at a large party. They said hello to each other but didn't talk much beyond that. Later, when Lisa thought about Kelly, she no longer felt hurt or annoyed, only sad. What she remembered was that she and Kelly had had good times together, and she missed their friendship. But she didn't follow up. Too much time had gone by, and it felt too awkward to call Kelly at that point. That was it. They never saw each other again.

The baby self had screwed up another friendship.

Lisa was not wrong to feel used, taken advantage of, hurt that she always had to be the initiator. It was true, as she sadly found out, that if not for her effort, the relationship would not have gone forward. But there was another reality as well. Whenever Lisa and Kelly got together, they had a good time. They enjoyed each other's company. And both valued the friendship. But in at least one respect they were quite different. Lisa was organized; she planned and took initiatives. Kelly was much more passive, allowed life to come to her, and was fortunate that she could get away with that. She was this way with everybody. Lisa was right: Kelly was spoiled. But she liked Lisa, and they did have a good time together—and this was what Lisa's baby self seemed to lose sight of.

What if someone told us that we could have a friend with whom we would always have a good time, but who had congenital phoneophobia and was thus unable to call anyone first? Most of us wouldn't have a problem, because we would see it as a flaw in the other person that had nothing to do with us. But since the baby self takes everything personally, it swiftly turned Kelly's behavior into a put-down.

She doesn't call because she doesn't think much of me. She doesn't really like me; she can't be bothered.

As always, there is another way of looking at it.

Kelly is self-centered. That's who she is. It has nothing to do with me. She's just not that reliable. If I want to have a relationship with her, I'll have to put up with her being self-centered. Or I can end the relationship. It's my choice.

Bad behavior by other people is about them, not about us. It is their flaw. We can either put up with it or not.

A Relationship at Work Gone Bad

What happens when a work relationship turns sour? A special problem exists with relationships in the workplace because of their dual nature (personal and business). This combination can get a little tricky. Often at work, the business relationship must necessarily continue even when the personal relationship fails. But the baby self in us does not easily let go of the personal connection once established, for when a friendship goes awry, good feelings invariably turn to hurt and anger.

Marianne had been working at Johnson and Jordan, a large public relations firm, for about a year when Anya started there. Marianne and Anya became friends. They had little contact with each other outside of work, but at work they were close, talking openly about their lives and the myriad ins and outs of what went on at Johnson and Jordan. Also, their jobs had them in frequent contact. Marianne worked on the ideas for a number of accounts where Anya was the main contact person with the clients. Both women were ambitious, wanting to move up in the company hierarchy, but so far their individual ambitions had not posed a problem for their relationship. Marianne's work friendship with Anya was one of the things she liked best about her job. But then one day she was at lunch with Jonah, another work friend.

"I'm sorry to hear that you and Wayne are having problems."

"Who said that?" asked Marianne, surprised that Jonah knew anything about her problems with her husband.

"Oh, I'm sorry. I guess I shouldn't have said anything, but Anya didn't say it wasn't for public knowledge."

Later: "Anya, why did you tell Jonah about me and Wayne? You know that was something I didn't want people at the office to know."

Anya seemed very contrite. "I'm sorry. It just popped out when I was talking to Jonah. I didn't realize that I wasn't supposed to say anything."

Marianne decided to believe Anya but was a little uneasy, as she remembered distinctly telling Anya not to mention her problems with Wayne to anybody else.

About two weeks later, in a meeting with John Warneke, her immediate supervisor at Johnson and Jordan, John said to her, "It's too bad that Darnell Davidson [a very successful author of self-help books who was a former client] left us. I hope you can figure out what in your approach turned him off."

"What?"

"Anya explained to me how Davidson said that the presentation of his last book seemed to him 'uninspired.' "

Marianne felt as if she'd been slapped. Both she and Anya knew that Anya had been the problem. From the start, Anya had rubbed Darnell Davidson the wrong way. If he had used the word "uninspired," he had been referring to his increasing distaste for Anya, not to Marianne's ideas. But Anya's description to their boss made it sound as if it were all Marianne's fault.

Later: "How could you say that to John?"

"He must have taken it the wrong way. Frankly, I don't remember exactly what I said—it was more than a month ago—but I certainly didn't blame you."

This time, Marianne did not believe Anya. She was upset. How could her friend say something to her boss that cast her in a bad light? Why would Anya do that?

Then, a few days later as they were waiting for the elevator, John Warneke said to Marianne, "I'm sorry you're not happy at Johnson and Jordan."

"That's not true. I am happy."

"Oh," said John, "I must have misunderstood."

Marianne knew exactly where that had come from. A week before, Marianne had been unhappy about a number of things and had been talking with Anya. She'd said that she was depressed and that, at the moment, her job seemed depressing, too.

This time she really confronted Anya. "How could you? You knew it would make me look bad. I thought we were friends."

"We *are* friends," said Anya.

"How can I trust you to tell you anything? I thought we were friends."

"We are friends," Anya insisted.

Marianne was very upset. She didn't understand.

Over the next few months, there were a number of confrontations at work between Marianne and Anya, most of them started by Marianne. They would disagree on some point, and Marianne would start in.

"Anya, you don't like my idea? You're just looking to find flaws in everything I suggest, aren't you? Anything you can do to make me look bad, isn't that it? I thought we had been friends. I can't believe you would have done this to me."

"You keep making a big thing out of nothing. Maybe I let some stuff slip I shouldn't have. But get over it."

"Maybe once, but it wasn't a slip."

"You're really getting to be impossible, Marianne."

And they would both get angry, raising their voices to the point that others in the office noticed.

In the end, their boss intervened, and it was decided—because both were good workers—to move Anya to a different department. As a result, Marianne and Anya had little further contact. But Marianne now had a reputation at work of being temperamental.

Once Marianne realized that Anya was a snake, why did she have to end up hurting herself by getting into arguments with her at work?

This is a sad story, for Marianne's baby self was not doing anything wrong. Indeed, it was doing something right. Marianne had allowed her baby self to enter into her relationship with Anya. She was open, trusting, and spontaneous, and she had been rewarded with a relationship that she genuinely enjoyed and valued. But it turned out that Anya was not a good friend. The very parts of herself that Marianne brought to the friendship that made it rewarding—her openness and spontaneity—were used against her. The friendship was ruined.

The baby self dies hard. Once Marianne recognized that Anya was a snake, she could not simply call off her baby self and send it back to its corner. It's not easy to shift gears just like that, to suddenly be formal and businesslike with someone to whom you were close. But this was what Marianne needed to do.

This kind of shift involves real loss. Marianne's baby self had invested in the relationship and was not about to simply let go of Anya as a nurturing source. Past any anger or hurt that Marianne felt toward Anya—the baby self is good at anger and hurt—needed to come that other feeling, the one the baby self is not good at: sadness. *Anya was my friend, and I really liked our friendship. Now I don't have that friendship anymore. And that makes me very sad.*

As long as Marianne's baby self refused to accept the reality that the friendship was gone, she would keep coming back to her hurt at Anya's betrayal.

How could you? I thought we were friends. How could you do this?

Only when the sad truth was fully accepted would "How could she?" become, *She did.*

What should you do when a good work relationship turns bad? You have to ask yourself over and over again, *Is my good relationship at an end? Is it over for good?* And when the answer is *yes,* then you can make the necessary switch to a purely business relationship. It is a loss, but a necessary one.

Chapter 10

I Want to Control Everything and Everybody

*G*od grant me the serenity to accept the things I cannot change, the courage to change the things I can, and the wisdom to know the difference.

The above is the well-known Serenity Prayer. The baby self did not write that prayer.

The baby self says: *I want to control everything and everybody always.*

Annette had been divorced from Fred for four years.

"I want to watch *Road Rangers*," demanded Annette's seven-year-old son, Kyle, one Tuesday evening.

"No, of course not, Kyle," said his mother. "No way am I going to let you watch that stuff." (The program contained a fair amount of violence.)

"But Dad lets me watch it when I'm over at his house."

"Absolutely not."

"But at Dad's I can."

The next evening, Annette called her ex. "Fred, is it true that you let Kyle watch *Road Rangers*?"

"What business is it of yours?"

"It's totally inappropriate content for a seven-year-old boy. And besides, it completely undermines what I am doing when he is with me. Or was that your point?"

"You know what's one of the great things about being divorced, Annette? I don't have to listen to you." And Fred hung up the phone.

The next day, Annette again called Fred.

"Is this about television programs?"

"Yes, I need to talk to you. We need to—" But Fred had already hung up.

Annette wrote Fred a long letter in which she reasonably and clearly spelled out why *Road Rangers* was not good for Kyle and why it was important that she and Fred, as Kyle's parents, back each other up.

Two days later, after a visit to his father's, Kyle repeated: "Dad said he just wanted you to know that he threw your letter in the trash. Can I watch *Road Rangers*?"

Annette called her lawyer, who said that he could write a letter to Fred or to Fred's lawyer, but that if she actually wanted to go to court about it, it would cost her money, and the court would almost certainly choose not to intervene about the TV watching.

There may be parts of your life about which you care very much but over which others have control. It can be very frustrating. Our baby self tries to control everything, but the mature self asks one question: *Is this a piece of the world over which I actually have any control?*

If the answer is yes, then trying to bring about change makes sense. But if not, the only wise thing to do is back off.

Hard as it may be for Annette, there is a consolation. When Kyle is with her, she is in charge. And in fact, if she stands firm about Kyle's not watching *Road Rangers* at her house, Kyle will swiftly drop the "But Dad lets me" for more successful ploys.

"But everybody in my class watches it, so if I don't, I won't be popular."

———

Caesar and Mack were carpenters who for a number of years had been working together for Jennings and Jennings, a big building contractor, installing kitchens and bathrooms in new and remodeled homes. Both Caesar and Mack were very good at what they did. Mack, however, was a heavy marijuana user; he never smoked when they worked but was high virtually all his other waking moments. The marijuana use did not seem to affect his work except for one thing, which may or may not have been related to the marijuana. Mack regularly showed up twenty to thirty minutes late for their jobs, which meant that Caesar often had to start without him. Jennings and Jennings either didn't notice or didn't care. The work the two men did was invariably high quality. But clients commented regularly, especially when Caesar and Mack were remodeling.

"If your friend showed up earlier, you would be out of here sooner and we wouldn't have to be inconvenienced."

Caesar sometimes complained to Mack, "I have to take their shit because of you, and besides, it's not fair to me that I have to work that extra amount of time when you're not here yet."

But Mack never changed.

Greg, a dentist, got home two hours later than usual.

"Denise drives me crazy. I had to stay two hours after work just to straighten out some of the billing."

"I told you, you should fire her," said his wife, Luanne.

"But what's she going to do? She's sixty-three. She needs the money, and she needs work. Since Maurice died five years ago, she's lost a lot."

"Greg, that's not your problem. She's lost you money. You know that. And she's not going to get any better."

"I'm just not comfortable letting her go."

"But that's not fair to me. Our money is tight, and as long as you keep Denise, you're throwing money away."

"I know, but I just can't do it."

"Well, you have to do it."

But Greg did not.

———————

Being unable to control others can be difficult, particularly when you are right and they are wrong. The other person is causing a problem that seems avoidable, if only they would listen to you. But your baby self has an especially hard time accepting the unhappy reality: If they don't listen, there is nothing you can do about it.

Annette can keep calling her ex, writing him letters, talking to her lawyer.

Caesar can keep complaining to Mack.

Luanne can keep complaining to her husband.

But they are trying to control others over whom they have no control.

"What's this?" said Luanne as she approached her front door that evening. Sitting on the welcome mat was a device that looked very much like a remote control. There was also a little instruction booklet explaining that the device was a husband controller and showing how to use it.

"This is weird," said Luanne, holding the device in her hand.

That night when Greg got home he seemed upset.

"I can't believe it. It was awful. I fired Denise. I don't know what got into me."

So far, no such controllers have actually been invented.

Rule: *It's okay to try to control other people. Just don't be too surprised if it doesn't work and they just get mad at you.*

Our Good Advice and How Nobody Seems to Want It

There's another terrible problem with people: Not only do they not take advantage of our excellent and very helpful advice, they often seem to *resent* it.

"Excuse me."

"Yes?"

"Do you like getting advice?"

"No, of course not, who does?"

"How about good advice?"

"It depends."

"It depends on what?"

"If it's about tips on really good stocks, yes; otherwise, no."

"How about advice on stuff you're doing wrong?"

"Are you crazy? Wait a minute, I forgot. Good little inexpensive restaurants. I like advice on that, too."

Bob and Selena went out to dinner. Selena was driving.

"Oh, for chrissakes, Selena, didn't you see that car?"

"Aren't you going a little slow? You know we don't have to go quite this slow, sweetheart. The speed limit says forty miles an hour."

"Selena, you took that corner a little wide, didn't you?"

Whenever I drive with Selena, I'm a nervous wreck. I'm surprised she doesn't get into accidents. I'm tense the whole time she's driving.

This is an obvious one. If Bob hates Selena's driving, he has a number of acceptable options:

1. He can drive.
2. He can refuse to ride with Selena.
3. He can ride with Selena and shut up.

Or:

4. He can ride in the trunk.

Not an option: Drive with Selena and criticize everything she does.

Unless others are doing exactly what you want them to, your baby self cannot just sit back and watch. Advice has to be *offered*. Give it freely, which means don't invest too much in whether or not they follow it. It is important to accept the fact that others may or may not wish to follow your very good advice, especially when you are trying to help or teach. The best learning occurs when the learner participates fully in the process. Unfortunately, our baby self has a way of screwing this up.

Jason's dad enjoyed cooking. One Sunday afternoon, he proposed that Jason help him make oatmeal raisin cookies, following a recipe on the oatmeal carton. This was the first time that Jason's dad suggested that he and Jason cook together.

"No, Jason, you have to stir harder. The butter and sugar aren't getting mixed enough. . . . Still even harder. . . . Jason, that's way too much oatmeal. The recipe says two cups. You don't need more than that. . . . Flatter, much flatter. The gobs of dough you're putting on the cookie sheet are too big. They won't get completely cooked in the middle. . . . No, Jason, they have to be the same size. Try to even the amount of dough for each cookie."

Each of Jason's dad's suggestions was correct. If Jason had made the cookies the way he had been doing it, they would not have come out nearly as well as they did.

"These look great," said Jason's dad as they took the cookies out of the oven.

The first time that Jason cooked with his father was the last time, which was too bad. For years, Jason's dad wondered why his son didn't share his enthusiasm for cooking.

In the face of too much correction, the learner becomes passive, letting the teacher be fully in charge ("Fine, whatever you say, Dad"), basically dropping out of the learning process; or else the learner resists, still wanting to have ownership of the process. This is the better response, but it has obvious problems:

"I don't see why I have to stir more. I stirred enough. It's mixed enough."

"No, Jason, look at it. There are still big clumps of butter."

"I don't see them."

"Look, right there."

"Dad, it looks fine."

"Well, it's not."

The cookie baking could become combative—a power struggle—with either or both participants becoming angry and frustrated.

It would have been best for Jason's dad to make a couple of comments at most but accept that the cookies might come out less than perfect. Jason would learn from his mistakes, but he would also feel that they were his cookies.

"Dad, they're kinda raw in the middle."

"We can cook them some more. But next time if you make them flatter when you first put them in, they get cooked all the way through."

"Yeah, next time I'll make them real flat. It was fun anyway."

There is a fine line between giving too little instruction and giving too much. But if you are the teacher and you want learning to occur, your students have to feel that they are in charge of what they are trying to do.

Trust

The baby self's need to control does the most damage with respect to the issue of trust.

Mitch and Wanda had been living together for over a year. Prior to their relationship, Mitch had a four-year relationship with Sofia. Sofia had been the one to break up. Sofia currently had a new boyfriend, but Wanda knew that sometimes Mitch and Sofia talked on the phone.

"We're just friends," Mitch explained.

Mitch liked to go out on Thursday nights to a regular poker game at his friend Trevor's. One Thursday, Wanda called Trevor's to remind Mitch to ask Trevor if they could borrow his Rototiller over the weekend. Trevor answered the phone and said there was no poker game that night and that Mitch was not there.

Mitch got home around his regular poker night time, and Wanda confronted him immediately.

"Where were you? I called Trevor's and you weren't there."

Mitch explained that when he went to pick up Randy, Randy had said that Trevor had just called to say no one else was coming and there wouldn't be enough people for a game. He and Randy decided to go to a movie instead. This was completely true. But a seed of doubt had been planted.

Is he secretly seeing Sofia?

Wanda found herself making excuses to check up on Mitch when he went out on Thursdays. She would call Trevor's:

"Mitch, I'm going crazy. I can't find my checkbook. Have you seen it anywhere around the apartment?"

"Honey, I hate to do this to you again, but could you pick up milk on your way home at the RediMart? I'm sorry, I didn't realize, but we're totally out."

"I know this could wait until later, but I'm beginning to get aggravated. Did you decide whether you want to go over to Stanley's Saturday night? I really should call him."

Wanda began questioning Mitch extensively about what went on with his phone calls with Sofia. Mitch, who was not seeing Sofia secretly, started to become irritated with Wanda's constant suspicion. The relationship became seriously strained.

But Mitch and Wanda stayed together. Realizing that his phone contacts with Sofia were a major problem for Wanda, Mitch stopped them altogether. He wanted to preserve his relationship with Wanda. Gradually, Wanda stopped worrying about Sofia. But it does not always work out that way.

There is one important rule about trust: *If you keep up regular surveillance as a means of establishing trust, you will* never *trust.* Only by yielding total control, by allowing for the possibility of betrayal and seeing that it does not occur over time, can you ever experience trust.

A stark difference between the mature self and the baby self is that the mature self will tolerate uncertainty. We cannot control everything. Often in life circumstances do not work out as we wish, but they work out a whole lot better when our baby self's need to remove all possible anxiety does not destroy precisely what it seeks to achieve.

This book is about letting go. And letting go is about trust. Trust that even though you do not manage every aspect of your life, the world won't collapse around you. Trust that in the end, people will like you rather than scorn you. Trust that if you let go, those you love won't leave forever.

A Simple Life Strategy

Having read this book you should now be able to back off when necessary.

Henry and Tanya had a fairly heated argument that seemed to have ended. Except apparently it hadn't.

"Tanya, there's just one more thing I have to say and then I'll shut up. I promise."

"Henry, what would Dr. Wolf say?"

"He'd say I'm not supposed to. But just one more thing, please. It's really important to clear things up."

"What will happen if you tell me this really important thing?"

"You'll probably get mad and it won't clear up anything—like always."

"Yeah?"

"But I have to tell you. I have to make you understand."

"What would Dr. Wolf say?"

"This is *really* hard. It is . . . I guess I'll go watch TV."

"That was good, Henry."

"Maybe I'll call Gary. Hello Gary. It's me, Henry."

"What's up?"

"I have to tell you one thing."

"Sure."

"She can criticize my brother, Kenny, all she wants, but God forbid I say one word about her sister, Jill."

"What are you talking about?"

"Thanks, I just had to tell somebody."

"I still don't know what you're talking about."

"Thanks a lot, buddy. Bye."

Controlling the baby self and shutting up is not always easy, but it does work best.

ABOUT THE AUTHOR

ANTHONY E. WOLF, PH.D., is a practicing clinical psychologist and the author of many bestselling books, including the recognized classic *Get Out of My Life, but First Could You Drive Me and Cheryl to the Mall?: A Parent's Guide to the New Teenager*. He has worked with adults, children, and families for more than thirty years and lectures widely on family issues. He lives in Suffield, Connecticut. Visit his website at AnthonyWolf.com.

ABOUT THE TYPE

This book was set in Bodoni, a typeface designed by Giambattista Bodoni (1740–1813), the renowned Italian printer and type designer. Bodoni originally based his letter forms on those of the Frenchman Fournier, and created his type to have beautiful contrasts between light and dark.